Aber publishing

Books to Improve Your Life

Choose Happiness

Ten steps to bring the magic back into your life

D0551873

Steve Wetton

ABER

© 2007 by Steve Wetton

ISBN: 978-1-84285-098-5

First published in 2007 by Aber Publishing.
PO Box 225, Abergele, LL18 9AY, United Kingdom.

Website: http://www.aber-publishing.co.uk

Typeset by Vikatan Publishing Solutions, Chennai, India
Printed and bound in Europe
Aber Publishing is a division of Studymates Limited

Dedication

Thanks to tv presenter Matthew Wright and psychic Jayne Wallace who gave me the final push I needed on '*The Wright Stuff*'.

And special thanks to my nephew Louca Hepburn and my cousin's wife Christine Reeves, without whose help and encouragement I would have finished this book a whole lot quicker – but never got it published.

Contents

Why I Wrote This Book

At the age of twenty-nine, I was jobless, homeless, divorced, without a single qualification and on the verge of suicide. That's when a devastating tragedy, followed by a strange happening, caused me to turn my life around. I started reading books on self-help and following some of the procedures they described and good things began to happen.

Thirty-five years later, they're still happening. The writing of this book is just the latest example. And for most of those years I've been living my dream: teaching; writing; conducting workshops; speaking to groups and loving it. Positive thinking changed my life completely. It can do the same for you.

There's nothing terribly difficult about it (not the way I see it anyway) no complicated theories to grapple with – no harsh regimes to follow and it can be fascinating just to learn about it.

Introducing the Cosmic Equal Opportunities Scheme

There *is* an element of mystery involved but you don't have to believe in 'magic' to get results. The 'magic' works anyway – whether you believe in it or not! It's a kind of cosmic equal opportunities scheme. And on one-level it's just commonsense. You learn how to behave better – you get better results. It can be as simple as that.

The strange happening that started it all for me, which I took to be a sign from a 'higher power', may have been nothing more than an amazing coincidence. Maybe I just 'fooled' myself into becoming a happier and 'better' person. But does that really matter?

Writing this book is something I've wanted to do for a long time now. I held back because I wasn't sure I could add much to what's already been written on the subject. It's only recently that I started wondering if a book that didn't attempt to break new ground but gave a very personal account of how it worked for me, was 'different' enough.

Someone who heard me speak at a recent writers' event said I have the knack of making a speech to a hundred people seem like a friendly chat. She said how delighted she'd been to realise how much information she'd taken-in without really being aware of it at the time. That's the kind of effect I'll be trying to produce with this book. It's written as a series of anecdotes about the things that have happened to me on my journey of discovery.

Some things were funny and exciting – others heartbreakingly poignant and puzzling. I simply tell about the techniques that worked for me without always trying to explain *why* they worked. The truth is I don't *know* why they worked. They just did. But through it all there's a pattern that convinced me that no matter how difficult the road became I was always heading in the 'right' direction.

You might be wondering if I ever arrived at my destination. The answer is, that I didn't have to. I was there all the time. I just didn't know it. It's a bit like taking a trip around the world. It starts on the day you set-off and doesn't end when you reach the furthest point. It carries on until the circle is completed – just like life itself.

Enjoying the journey is everything. If you learn just one thing from this book, that can change your life for the better, I'll consider it a job well done.

Is it for you?

I wrote this book with two groups of people in mind. Firstly there are those potential readers who've already given this subject a try and wouldn't mind comparing their experiences to my own.

And secondly, that much larger group of people who don't necessarily want to win a gold medal at the Olympics, or earn more money than they know what to do with but just improve the quality of their lives in general. In other words they are people who want to be happier, healthier and more fulfilled.

Many years ago I had a friend, called Stan Birkinshaw, who taught self-defence techniques. He was a brilliant motivator and used to say to his new and sometimes nervous pupils, 'I won't lie to you. I can't turn a budgerigar into an eagle but I *can* help you to become the most effective budgerigar you're ever likely to be.'

He wasn't talking about things on a purely physical level of course. He was encouraging quiet self-confidence and preparedness. A willingness to make the very best of whatever you have despite your self-perceived limitations. That's what this book is all about. Learning not to settle for less than you're really worth. Isn't that something well worth considering?

What is positive thinking anyway?

I'd always assumed that most people would automatically understand what positive thinking actually means. Then one night I had to leave my weekly five-a-side football session a bit earlier than usual as I'd agreed to talk to a group of people who were all recovering from heart attacks. I was going to tell these group members how a change of attitude as well as a change of habits might help their recovery.

(And please note: I am now sixty-eight and *still* taking part in this hectic sport, with people less than half my age, so it should be pretty obvious I try to practise what I preach.)

Anyway, one of my younger soccer friends shook his head at me in mild disbelief and said, 'You seem a nice enough bloke to me Steve. So why are you teaching people how to be more ruthless and get what they want at all costs? Especially when that's probably what caused them to have their heart attack in the first place.'

At first I laughed because I thought he was joking. But he was deadly serious, 'Is that what you think positive thinking is all about?' I asked but before he could reply another player butted-in with: 'Of course it's not. It's the exact opposite. Steve's telling them to bury their heads in the sand and pretend everything's okay – when it isn't.'

And *he* wasn't joking either. These were two totally opposing views and both of them wrong. (In my opinion!) Yet these were by no means ill-informed people. They were both intelligent, sensible and, I would have thought, pretty positive types anyway.

I realised that if they could hold such differing views on the subject then so could millions of others. I was in a hurry so I could only give a quick off the cuff and very brief definition.

'Positive thinking,' I said, 'Is trying to get the best out of any situation, for everyone concerned, however bad things might appear at that moment.'

If I'd had more time I might have added something Dale Carnegie (one of the great pioneers of positive thinking) wrote in a book called '*How To Stop Worrying And Start Living*'. (Cedar Books World's Work Ltd. 1948)

I'll paraphrase here because Dale was quoting someone else (who was quoting someone else) but in essence here it is: 'If life hands you a lemon – make lemonade.' To me that's positive thinking in a nutshell. As I implied earlier it's a pretty simple concept when you get right down to it. Nothing the average person can't understand and quickly start using to their own and everybody else's advantage. So why not give it a try?

Steve Wetton

steve@aber-publishing.co.uk

1 How It All Started for Me

I WOKE-UP THAT PARTICULAR MORNING WITH a sickening hangover and the ridiculous hope that it might all have been a nightmare. Maybe my best friend, his step-son, his young daughter, his brother and his brother's wife hadn't all been killed in a dreadful road accident, and their bodies weren't lying in a hospital mortuary in France?

Maybe another member of the family – a brother-in-law still only in his thirties – hadn't really died of a heart attack shortly after hearing the news? It all seemed so horrendous and surreal but it was true. Only a day or so earlier I'd received a postcard from my friend saying what a wonderful time they were having, travelling through Spain on their way to France before coming back to the UK. It ended with the words 'See you soon.' Now only his wife had survived the crash and how was she ever going to cope?

I turned to face the empty pillow next to me and that's when I realised it wasn't all a dream. My wife, Maureen, wasn't there as I'd hoped she might be. The complete silence in the house reminded me that our son's bedroom was empty too. Maureen, our son Robert and me were supposed to have gone on that tragic holiday with my friend and his family. It was something I'd really been looking forward to.

Then shortly before the holiday my wife had taken our son and left me. It had come as a shock but not a surprise. I'd had a wonderful wife, an attractive woman with a lovely personality, and a son to be proud of, but I had been pretty useless as a husband and role model. I drank too much, still chased after other women and worst of all, I was a bully who was sometimes violent. I now think this was all because of my deep unhappiness but I was too angry to realise that at the time – besides which there seemed to be no reason for it.

I'd always been a fairly popular sort of person. People who didn't really know me saw me as easy-going and friendly. They didn't realise that deep inside I was struggling to make some kind of sense out of my life. I hated all the jobs I'd ever had – over thirty at that point and I was still only twenty-nine. Even though I was young, fit and healthy

I could see no future ahead of me. I didn't know what I wanted to do or where I wanted to be. *I WAS LOST.*

As I lay there that morning I wondered why I, who was so unhappy, was still alive – yet my friend and five other members of his family were dead. It just didn't make any sense.

Then I noticed something strange. On the bedclothes were what looked like bird droppings? As crazy as it now seems that gave me a moment of hope. Maybe it *was* all a dream after all? For the sight of the bird droppings inside my bedroom wasn't just an unusual sight – there was a link to another incident and that meant that this sight was significant – extremely significant.

It had happened a few hours earlier, when my best friend's mother had told me about something incredibly strange. She'd been working in her kitchen when a sparrow had flown in and perched on a worktop above the washing machine. She'd been startled by this – particularly since the washing machine was working and making a lot of noise. She tried to shoo the bird away out of the house and back outside but at first it had no effect. She tried again.

This time the bird seemed to look steadily into her eyes for a moment before flying away. That's when the effect hit her. She felt faint and stumbled into a chair overcome by the sudden feeling that something really dreadful had happened.

She said to me later that she somehow 'knew' that the bird was acting as a kind of spiritual messenger. And she knew with certainty she was about to get some terrible news. This was at a time when the accident had already happened but before anyone here in Britain knew anything about it.

Birds and spiritual messages

It was the first time I had ever heard about unusual sightings of birds being connected to spiritual messages. And now – just a few hours later – there appeared to be bird droppings on my own bedclothes. The whole thing seemed too weird to be true.

I opened my eyes again. The bird droppings were still there and they seemed real enough. I looked around the room. A small pane in the window was open but there were net curtains across it, as well as thicker curtains that almost covered the whole window space. Why would a bird struggle through a window and then past two lots of curtains into a room where someone was sleeping? And why on this very morning? Nothing like this had ever happened to me before and it hasn't happened again since. That spans a time-scale of well over half a century. Some coincidence if that's all it was!

Then I saw the bird, cowering in terror as it flapped around in a state of near-exhaustion trying to find its way back outside. I got a lightweight towel from the bathroom and draped it over the terrified bird. That made it possible for me to scoop the bird up without actually squeezing it too much.

I didn't want to struggle to open the window a little wider, with one hand and then try to push the bird though the small opening so I took it downstairs, opened the front door and gently let the little bundle fall open.

The bird swooped up to the sky in a graceful arc. I watched it disappear and felt an overwhelming moment of peace. I suddenly knew what my friend Bryan's mother had been talking about when she'd told me of her certainty about receiving a message.

I too had now received a message. I hadn't seen words of gold written in the clouds and I hadn't heard any strange voices but I just knew what Bryan was saying to me at that moment.

He was telling me I had no reason to mourn for him or the children or the other adults who had died. They were being looked after in a 'better' place. It was me and all the people left behind, who I should start to care more about. If I didn't I was just wasting my time on Earth. I might have been imagining this, I'll admit, but it didn't *feel* like that. My whole body had relaxed, the turmoil in my mind had gone and so had the hangover. I was calm and rational and focussed.

I knew then that I had choices to make. I could carry-on treating other people with contempt and live a miserable life. I could take my own life without a care for the effect this would have on my son, all the rest of my relatives and the people who'd never given-up on me. Or, I could start trying to do something worthwhile. Looked at like that it wasn't too difficult a choice. It hasn't always been easy and I've made lots of mistakes but I've never doubted for a moment that I made the right choice that day.

Not that there was a sudden and miraculous improvement in my circumstances: quite the reverse. Shortly after this moment of revelation things got even worse for me. I had wondered if the tragedy involving our friends would somehow bring my estranged wife and me back together again. It didn't. She was already feeling terrible and this only made her feel worse. She must have felt that everything to do with me was a disaster and she had to get away. She decided to start divorce proceedings on the grounds of cruelty.

I still feel ashamed when I think of this. How could I have been cruel to someone who'd once been head over heels in love with me and wasn't embarrassed to show it? A woman who'd asked for so little in return? Just to be treated kindly – with the love and respect she deserved. I'd had it in my power to make her really happy and I'd callously and stupidly turned the chance down. And it wasn't as if I didn't love her too. There was no doubt in my mind that I did. So nothing made any sense to me.

A few weeks later I was sacked from the job I had lost all interest in. Then I was forced out of the house. It was a three-bedroomed council house and I was a man living on his own. I was no longer entitled to be there. My parents were kind enough to let me move back to live with them.

It couldn't have been easy for them. Once upon a time they'd had big hopes for me. Despite getting no academic qualifications at my secondary modern school (this was before the days of the UK's school 'O' an 'A' level examinations) I'd done well there – both in my classwork and in sports. I'd played football for Derby Boys and for the county too. The England Schoolboys' selectors had even considered me.

I had then signed amateur forms for Derby County and later married this lovely girl they liked and respected and had a healthy son with her. In their eyes I'd had so much going for me – until, for some inexplicable reason I'd thrown it all away.

Now I wasn't just back at square one but some place even further back than that. I was an unemployed, unqualified, unhappy mess who'd just lost his wife, his best friend, his job and his house.

I'm not sure that I told my parents about the incident with the bird. I probably thought they'd assume I'd finally flipped altogether and they had enough to contend with. And despite my decision about trying to live a better life it wasn't proving easy. I was still drinking too much alcohol, still getting involved with various women and still getting myself into the odd fist-fight – usually with somebody bigger and stronger than me or perhaps somebody who was part of a gang who all happened to be together at that point.

But it was about this time that a friend (my cousin Ken actually) gave me a book on positive thinking and said, 'What have you got to lose?' He was right. Although I hadn't entirely forgotten my thoughts of suicide it was now only 'pencilled-in' as a vague possibility. It certainly wasn't written on my forward-planner in indelible ink.

I read the book. I cut down on my drinking and womanising. I stopped trying to give people unwanted boxing lessons. I read more books. I'm still doing it. Some books I like and others I don't. I'm sure you'll feel the same if your interest develops as mine did. I might add that if somebody like me (I mean as I *was*) can make positive thinking work for him then *anybody* can.

Please don't see this as a challenge and try to prove me wrong! Be patient. There'll be plenty of challenges coming along anyway and I want you to enjoy them.

And if anybody ever tells you that a leopard never changes its spots ask them if they've ever read Hans Anderson's story, *The Ugly Duckling*.

How I felt 'guided' to write this book

I made my New Year resolutions for 2006 in the middle of February. I've always been a bit slow to make decisions and this was a very important one that needed mulling over. In fact I'd been mulling it over for five or six years! It was all about the writing of this book. (Well – not exactly *this* book. A book on positive thinking.)

I had already written a very detailed outline and a proposal for such a book. It was to be called; *Smile Your Way To Success* and two publishers had shown some initial interest. Oddly, I had then lost interest myself. Not the best start for someone wanting to inspire and motivate people I think you'll agree. And for a long while I couldn't understand *why* my interest had waned. Then it suddenly hit me. The ideas I'd outlined were not saying what I wanted them to say. In fact they were saying almost the exact opposite.

I was basically describing how to manipulate people. Not necessarily in a harmful way but not always in a 'caring' way either. And it wasn't what I'd done myself anyway. I wasn't being honest enough and telling how it *really* happened for me. I was mixing truth and theory in an effort to be more efficient and more helpful to a potential reader. I had also placed too much emphasis on material things: earning more money; buying a bigger house; having more expensive holidays and so on. It had been staring me in the face all the time. It was implicit in the title, *Smile Your Way To Success*. It sounded like a book specifically aimed at cowboy builders or dodgy double-glazing salesmen.

I had relegated the spiritual aspects of positive thinking to a couple of chapters near the end of the book. The most important things in my own life – the thoughts and feelings that had made such an impact on me – I had practically overlooked. I had been hoping to write a book that inspired and uplifted people, a book that filled them with delight. Instead I'd come-up with something as exciting as the instructions you get with a self-assembly kitchen unit. It was clear and efficient but there was no 'magic' at all.

And the minute I made that discovery a series of weird coincidences started to happen. At first I tried to ignore them because they made me feel a little uneasy but then I lost my fear and started to relish and look out for them. I won't go into to much detail here because I'm going to talk about meaningful coincidence (synchronicity) and about seemingly paranormal happenings, in a later chapter. I'll just cut to the final incident that really spurred me on.

The Wright Stuff on Five TV

I was watching Matthew Wright hosting his excellent tv show, *The Wright Stuff* , on the UK's Five tv station when it was announced that a psychic would be a guest on the show the following day. She was going to give readings to people by looking at a photograph and tuning-in to the person's voice over the phone. Without hesitation I sent a photograph of myself by email and included a question I'd like answered. (As requested along with the photograph.) My question was: 'I'm planning to write a book on positive thinking. Do you think it's the right thing to do?'

I wasn't at all sure what I hoped to get out of this and I'm not the kind of person who seeks publicity for it's own sake. It just seemed like yet another coincidence – that I should be watching daytime tv when I would normally be working – at a time when a psychic was involved. I had immediately felt a strong urge to give it a try.

But that evening I mentioned it to a writer friend who thought I was crazy. 'You're supposed to be writing a book telling other people how to be more positive and you're asking a complete stranger for advice?' she said. That's not going to impress many people.' I had to admit she might have a point. I decided not to mention it to anyone else for the time being.

Early the next morning I told my wife Pat (by now I'd long been re-married) about it as we lay in bed. She looked worried. She agreed with what my writer friend had said and was prepared to add her own thoughts. 'What's the point of getting publicity for a book you haven't even started writing? It could be over a year before a publisher even considers it and by then nobody will remember what you said on a tv phone-in. Plus,' she added, a bit more ominously, 'The psychic lady might think you're an idiot.'

'You think she could be *that* good?' I asked, trying to jolly things along and then said, 'Anyway – they'll get thousands of people sending emails so what's the chances that they'll. ...? And that's when the phone rang.

As it happened the psychic lady, Jayne Wallace, didn't think I was an idiot. (Or at least – she didn't say so!) She was very supportive. She immediately said something that impressed me. She said I needed to pay more attention to the spiritual aspects of my book – which of course is what I'd already decided myself. She had no way of knowing that because I'd barely said anything apart from asking my question.

She also said she thought I had psychic ability myself – which I wouldn't really argue about because I think it's something we *all* have to a greater or lesser extent (as you'll see as you go through this book).

I may even have confused her by asking a totally different question to begin with. I'd been feeling very nervous as I waited – phone in hand – for my turn to speak. And for no apparent reason, when Matthew Wright gave me a cheery greeting and said, 'Okay Steve, what's your question?' Instead of asking the question they were expecting I said, 'I am sixty-seven years of age and still not sure what I want to be when I grow-up.' I hadn't planned to say this. It just came out and it got a laugh from the studio audience and from Matthew himself who seemed a genuinely friendly man. He asked me if I was sceptical about psychics and I said I'd had some remarkable experiences with a relative who is psychic.

I then asked the question I was supposed to ask. Jayne rounded-off her comments by saying, 'I think you should write the book. You have lots of people willing to help – both in this world and in the spirit world too. So go for it.'

And at that point Matthew re-appeared to say, 'And if you *do* Steve, you can come on this show and talk about it. That's a promise.' And it didn't end there. The next phone-in caller, Gail from Glasgow, who sounded like a very nice lady indeed, was told by Jane to be more positive. She laughed and said, 'I'll have to buy a copy of Steve's book.'

This led Matthew to say, 'There you are Steve. You've already sold a copy of your book and had an invitation to come on this show – and that's before you've written a word. How lucky can you get?'

Again I felt a chill down my spine. Since I'd been praying and meditating for signs that I was on the right track it was almost as if God himself (or herself!) was looking down at me and saying, 'That's *it* Steve. If you're waiting for a telephone call from me – don't hold your breath.' I started writing the book.

2 Change Your Attitude

IF YOU'VE READ THIS FAR INTO the book I can imagine you pausing for a moment and thinking: 'Okay Steve that's not a bad start to your *autobiography* and I'm glad you managed to turn your life around – but I thought this was some kind of 'How To' book. So what's in it for me? What can I do *right now* to improve my life and give me more of this happiness, healthiness and fulfilment you mentioned at the beginning?'

Good question. (See – you're learning already. I'm impressed!) And I apologise if I got carried away there and went on about myself for a bit too long. But you can see how much this all means to me. I'm enthusiastic about life and I want you to feel the same. I've already mentioned several positive thinking techniques in passing: belief in a higher power; meaningful coincidence; acting on intuition; listening to your inner-signals and even receiving messages through psychic mediums. I realise I may have confused you by throwing such a lot into the mix right at the beginning.

But give it a bit of thought and I think you'll agree that almost everything I've said so far leads to one vital thing, a change in attitude. Basically it's as simple as that. That's what I did. Remember? And that's what all the examples and techniques in this book are really aimed at. So I'm now going to ignore all the things I tried that *didn't* work for me and concentrate on ones that *did*.

I've formed them into a ten-step process that I think follows a logical order of progression. But don't panic, this isn't some regimented programme for you to follow slavishly. These ideas are there for you to sample at your leisure. You might find yourself immediately attracted to some of them but turned-off by others and that's fine.

Any of the techniques mentioned can work to your benefit all by themselves or in various combinations. Choose the things you know you'll enjoy doing and keep an open mind on the others. There's no rush. Learning to be happier isn't a quick-fix – it's a way of life.

After the ten-step process I've added a final chapter called 'And Something Extra' which gives a few more examples of the strange things that have happened to me that *seem* to give evidence of a 'higher power' but which don't easily fit into any category. You may decide to ignore this chapter or you may read it out of curiosity.

As I've already implied there are no hard and fast rules here. I'm trying to entertain and stimulate you – not crush your creative spirit with a set of rules and regulations. So why not relax, read the whole book first (just out of curiosity perhaps) and then come back to this point and decide if you're ready to start trying out the techniques for yourself? It really is your choice.

That's why I called the book, **Choose** Happiness not Let **Me Force** Happiness Upon You. So here we go with the first step.

The benefits of choosing a 'good' attitude

You've probably heard this little story in one form or another. A man is thinking of moving from his home in the UK to live in Spain. He asks someone who's already done that, for advice. He says, 'Do you think I'd be happy living in Spain and would I get on well with the people there?' The person asks the man if he's happy in Britain and if he gets on well with the people living *there.*

'I hate it in Britain,' the man replies, 'It's always raining and the streets are full of criminals. I hate my neighbours as well – they are horrible people. That's why I want to get away.'

'Aah,' says the man being asked for advice, 'If that's the case I don't think you'd like it very much in Spain either.' He might well have added, 'Or anywhere else for that matter.'

I'm sure you get the point. The unhappy man really needed to change his *attitude* not merely his *circumstances*. He was living in Britain – a country which millions of people (including myself) feel very fortunate to have been born in. And he was unhappy here. Why – apart from general moans and groans?

He needed to stop feeling sorry for himself and sort out his personal problems *first*, not cause a whole lot of upheaval in his life, only to find he was still as miserable as ever (or even more so) because he'd taken his feelings with him and possibly found a lot of new things to moan about too. Despite what many (perhaps the majority) of people think this is the vital key to making meaningful changes to your life:

It makes more sense to change your attitude first and your circumstances second.

You may find that once you've changed your attitude your circumstances will *seem* to change to follow suit without you having to do very much about it. I know this may sound strange but I assure you it's something I've found to be true again and again. I'll give you a few examples of this:

The job interview

This first little story concerns one of my step-children. (From my second marriage.) She came back from a job interview one day practically dancing with joy. She'd not only been selected from dozens of other hopeful applicants to get the interview in the first place but she was now one of only two still in the running.

The two finalists had been invited to spend a whole day with the company – to give them more idea what the job entailed and of course to see how they managed to get along with the rest of the staff.

And that task went brilliantly too. My step-daughter told me and her mother she was certain she'd done well enough to get the job but when the letter arrived a day or so later it was bad news. The letter was very complimentary and said the choice had been terribly difficult. In the end it had come down to the fact that the other young lady had slightly better qualifications.

Our daughter was distraught. It certainly wasn't the time for me to point out the positives in the situation. The fact that she'd done so well to come a close second, out of dozens of other applicants, or that she'd gained a valuable experience in knowing how to conduct herself in a stressful situation.

Then I had a closer look at the letter. It ended with a request to keep her name on file in case another vacancy occurred. It said, 'Please let us know if this is acceptable to you.' My step-daughter uttered a few rather unladylike phrases as I tentatively pointed this out to her. Then she screwed the letter up, threw it in the rubbish bin and rushed up to her bedroom in tears. Her mother went after her.

I gave it a moment's thought, fished the letter out of the bin and went to my computer to type out an answer. I decided *not* to use a couple of the words my step-daughter had suggested. (Well I am supposed to be a creative writer!) I kept it brief and remembered all the 'good' things she had said about the company and the way she'd been treated during both interviews. I told no lies and didn't exaggerate. I simply wrote what I 'knew' my step-daughter would be able to write once she'd calmed down. (In a year or two!)

In the brief letter, pretending to be my step-daughter, I wrote that, although 'I' was deeply disappointed, I knew the other young lady would be able to do a good job for the company and wished them all well.

I ended by saying I'd love to be considered for any other vacancy they thought suitable. Then added that I was sure they'd understand I would be searching for other positions in the meantime.

I almost started practising my step-daughter's signature but thought better of it. I was already pushing things a *tiny* bit spiritually and I knew from experience I'd never gained anything substantial by trickery.

The next day she read what I'd written and, after a few minutes thought, agreed with it. She couldn't deny that the other young lady seemed very nice and had earned her 'victory' fairly. She signed the letter and sent it off, feeling a little bit better about the whole thing but not expecting to gain anything more than that.

But the very next day someone from the company phoned to say how impressed they'd all been by her sensible and optimistic attitude. They now thought she was too good a prospect to lose and had decided to do something they'd never done before. They were prepared to create a part-time job for her on the understanding that, if this went well, she would take over the job of someone who was due to leave in a few months time to start a family.

She took the part-time job. It did lead to a full-time position and she stayed with that company, for several years, before leaving to start a family of her own. A simple change of attitude followed by an even simpler follow-up action had helped to give her an almost instant change of fortune. And this was something that affected her life in a positive way, on a daily basis, for several years.

My 'early learning' days

I guess I was born lucky because I think I *always* knew the importance of having a positive attitude. This second example I'd like to tell you about happened before I'd even heard of positive thinking as a series of techniques. It was just something I 'knew' instinctively.

I was nineteen at the time and doing my national service in the army. I absolutely hated most of it. I hated being shouted at, told what to do, and generally treated like a robot. And I was a bit concerned that I might have to fight against, or even kill somebody, I didn't even know, and for reasons I wasn't exactly sure about. (No doubt a bit like many of our troops in world trouble-spots at the moment – except that they are all professionals and many of us were conscripts.)

But I was also excited about being on the strange and exotic island of Singapore and I was determined to enjoy being there as much as I could. The first meal I remember having in our military camp was served-up by Chinese cooks. Now in those days racism was rampant. Some (certainly not all) of the more gung-ho British squaddies were less than complimentary to people they considered to be part of an inferior race. (That is – anybody who wasn't white and English though some Scots and Welshmen were considered fairly acceptable.)

But anyway we lined-up with our plates ready to be filled, from a choice of things on offer and the two men ahead of me were immediately disparaging about the food and dismissive to the people serving it. The food looked and smelt pretty good to me. I said so and politely asked a question about a curry dish. A couple of the cooks looked at me warily and said very little.

Something similar occurred at the next meal and the one after that but I persisted in being pleasant and appreciative because I genuinely thought it was the right thing to do – not because I was trying to get something out of it. But guess what started to happen shortly afterwards? That's right – it isn't rocket science is it? I mysteriously started to get the leanest cuts of meat and the biggest portions of everything else.

On occasions I was even sometimes discreetly refused a dish I'd asked for and given something else instead. With just the hint of a smile from the server and a raised eyebrow to indicate I was being done a favour.

I spent over a year and a half in that camp and can't remember having a bad or unpleasant meal. More than once I was offered a packed lunch made-up from food left over from a meal to take with me to the beach and one Chinese civilian worker actually invited me to his wedding.

(It says something about the values of that time nearly fifty years ago and my own lack of confidence in certain situations – that I made an excuse and didn't go. I was afraid of being an outcast amongst some of my fellow soldiers.) I heard later that it had been a fabulous occasion with a vast variety of food to choose from and with friendly guests dressed in spectacular style. I was a fool to say no.

But what caused me to have a happier experience, in general, with the locals than many of my colleagues? Nothing more than a difference in attitude. And here's the silliest thing about it. It was *easier* to be pleasant and friendly, than sarcastic and hostile. And I know a cynical person might say I was manipulating people even if I didn't realise it but if that's true what harm was I doing? I was happier and so were the other people directly involved. The only ones not to benefit were the ones who'd done little to deserve it.

Why I didn't use this instinctive knowledge later on when I was busy destroying my first marriage and having one unhappy job after another I simply don't know. I guess I just have to admit that we all make mistakes and never reach a stage when we can relax and say, that's it – I'm perfect

The incredible power of a 'relaxed' attitude

Does having a 'good' attitude mean that you are more likely to get a good result? My answer is an unequivocal yes. This is easy to see on a commonsense level and one excellent positive thinking technique I can heartily recommend is about dealing with people in awkward situations. Instead of being drawn into an argument with somebody who might not even be directly involved with the problem (like a receptionist on a telephone switchboard for instance). You simply focus on the result you want to achieve – stay calm and polite – and virtually ignore everything that isn't leading to your desired goal.

I'm sure you know the kind of thing I mean. You are blazing with anger and determined to let somebody know about it. Maybe you've been sent a final demand for a bill you've already paid weeks earlier and somebody's now threatening you with court action over it?

You pick-up the phone and dial the number. Even if the person who answers your call is friendly and helpful you may *still* be tempted to let fly – saying things you may later regret. But if the person isn't that friendly but a bit impatient you can easily forget what you phoned about and get entangled in an argument about something else.

If you then forget what you were actually calling *about* and just start swapping insults, you have lost control of yourself and handed it over to the other person. You may 'win' this little skirmish. You might even feel a moment of satisfaction as you slam the phone down on some stranger whose parentage and level of intelligence you've just called into question.

But it doesn't take long for you to realise you've won the battle but lost the war. You haven't achieved whatever it was you were after. No only that but you may have left some innocent person (who was only trying to do their job and may have been feeling harassed) feeling suicidal. And is *that* something to feel good about?

And pretty soon you'll feel frustrated because you haven't settled anything or even clarified the situation. And that means you'll have to call again – only this time they'll be ready for you and probably not feel inclined to be helpful. You might even go through exactly the same procedure again.

Trust me on this. I really know what I'm talking about here. More than once I've phoned companies to discuss a problem and almost come to blows – over the phone! And once I actually went into the classified adverts office of a newspaper to follow-up on a phone call and things got so heated that somebody phoned the police and I narrowly avoided getting arrested.

And I had a legitimate point to make that eventually got me an apology and a re-print of something they'd got wrong. But you can imagine how many new friends I made in the process. And this may have had repercussions I couldn't have imagined at the time.

Years later, when I became a writer, I *needed* the good will of that newspaper. As it happens they proved to be pretty forgiving and have always been kind to me – but I was lucky and they could so easily have taken the opposite view.

But that was a minor annoyance compared to one of the stupidest things I ever did in this kind of situation, and I'm talking here about 'stupid' of gold-medal winning standards.

Ruining my own career

I'd been promised a promotion as a teacher and told not to tell anyone about it until a formal announcement was made. But when that moment came someone else got the promotion. It happened to be a colleague I really liked and who had every right to get the promotion but I lost my temper and accused my head-teacher of lying to me. I did this in front of witnesses. It upset everyone – including the totally innocent teacher who'd got the promotion and even a few pupils who happened to be in the vicinity.

I should have talked to the headmaster privately and listened to his reasons for changing his mind. Not only would that have been the 'right' thing to do but on a pragmatic level I would have been in a pretty strong position to get the next promotion on offer, or at least to get a great reference when it became appropriate.

I actually got on well with that headmaster and knew he valued me as a teacher. He would surely have felt guilty about what he'd done (or at least the way he'd done it) and would have wanted to make amends in some way. And it later turned-out that he had an excellent reason for giving the promotion to this other teacher. One I couldn't have argued over.

But once I'd insulted him in such a public manner there was no chance of me staying-on at that school. I still felt resentful and he, no doubt, felt embarrassed at having his authority undermined. (To be fair to him he actually asked me to stay-on.) But I felt that I just had to ask for a transfer. A moment of uncontrolled anger had wiped out four years of hard work.

I'd been really happy and successful at that school but ended-up in one where the atmosphere was much less friendly and where I was viewed with suspicion. My reputation as a hothead had preceded me and I was seen as a troublemaker. I felt I was never fully accepted by my new head-teacher who hadn't really wanted me there in the first place.

It's not difficult to see the connections between this example and the one I gave earlier regarding my daughter and her job application. She did the 'right' thing and landed herself several years of happiness in a career. I did the 'wrong' thing and swapped a great job with prospects – for a more difficult one with no prospects at all.

How the 'bad' effects can linger on

As crazy as it seems the effects of that bad decision, I made over thirty years ago are *still* not over. My teacher's pension is based on my past earnings in that profession and they stayed at the lower end of the scale for another eight years after my transfer. That means I was eventually awarded a much smaller pension than my colleagues, who went on to become head-teachers or whatever, and that pension will stay at that lower rate for the rest of my life.

That one moment of madness 'cost' me untold thousands of pounds and took me away from a position I loved and put me into one that was much more difficult. And as a teacher I never really got back into that really happy position again until I started teaching at Derby University many years later.

So no matter how angry you are about something you should never let your feelings get out of control. And if possible you prepare yourself *before* the event.

You decide exactly what you want to get out of any such situation and never let that thought leave your mind. If anyone is rude or aggressive towards you, you don't respond. You stay calm and focussed.

You just keep thinking – I want my money back – or I'm happy at this school and don't want to leave it – or whatever else it is you want. You're not interested in winning a personal argument. So you don't even acknowledge there's an argument going on. You stick to your purpose and focus on your goal. I know it works. Try it and see.

Attitude affects performance: A dramatic example

This idea of never losing your control, in order to be more effective, works in even the most highly charged situations. As a youngster I was a pretty good boxer and later I did judo and now Tai chi. In all of these sports the best performers are the ones who can control their anger and focus their intentions.

My judo instructor Stan (the one who talked about not being able to turn a budgerigar into an eagle) didn't only teach judo as a sport but also as a method of self-defence. One thing we practised was how to defend ourselves against a knife-attack. Stan's contention was that anyone using a knife as a weapon was unwittingly giving you an advantage by making his (or her) intentions very clear.

In other words, that person is not going to keep you guessing, as a trained boxer or martial arts expert would be able to do. (Should such a person have the need to do that in the first place. Which is very unlikely because one of the first things they learn about is self-control.) A knife-attacker is going to lunge at you with the knife. So you can focus all your attention on that one thing.

Not only that but the attacker is unlikely to have *trained* and practised to use a knife. He is more likely to be out of control. (Maybe this isn't so true nowadays but it certainly was forty years ago.)

Anyway, in our group we would practise defence against knife attacks and it was clear the instructor knew what he was talking about. When you were playing the part of the attacker it seemed almost impossible to score a 'hit' on somebody. You always came off second best.

You simply didn't know what your intended 'victim' was going to do so you had no defence against it. But there was always one nagging doubt and it was this: A real attacker was *fairly* unlikely to use a rubber knife. So how much difference would that make in a 'real' situation? The theory was excellent and it worked in what might be called 'rehearsals' but we all wondered if it would be 'alright on the night' as it were.

Then I was given a chance to find out. (I told you I was a lucky person!) It happened whilst I was working at a children's summer camp in America, when I was training to be a teacher. One lunchtime, in the dining area, a man I didn't know approached me in a threatening manner. It was something to do with a woman he considered to be his girlfriend. (No need to go into details here but I was divorced from my first wife by this time and hadn't done anything to be ashamed of on this occasion.)

Anyway, the jealous boyfriend thought I'd be frightened of him. (And he was right!) He was well built and muscular and altogether a tough-looking character. He asked me to step outside with him for a moment. I decided to keep cool, do as he asked and try to talk to him. But, once we got outside, it seemed he wasn't looking for friendly conversation. He just wanted to assert his authority in front of the many children who had followed us to form an audience.

He told me, in no uncertain terms, never to go anywhere near his girlfriend again. I politely asked him if that shouldn't be *her* decision – not his. His answer was to take a roundhouse swing at me. I blocked it easily and told him to calm down. He rushed at me with both arms flailing wildly.

I didn't have much space for manoeuvre because we were in a car-park and several vehicles hemmed us in as well as the bunch of excited young campers who had followed us to form themselves into an impromptu cheer-leading group in my support.

I blocked another punch but this time, automatically, pumped-out a short right hook to the man's jaw. He'd been moving on to it and it landed perfectly. He stopped short before stumbling to his knees. There was a shocked silence.

I was deeply embarrassed and offered the man my hand to help him up. And then the whole thing seemed to turn into a clip from a movie as he ignored my offer of help and pulled a knife from his back pocket. It was what Americans call a switch-blade and it flicked open. 'I'm going to kill you for that – you mother..' (expletive deleted) the man said. It was the kind of thing I'd seen lots of times in gangster movies. It really did seem surreal.

And for a moment I panicked. This wasn't a friend with a rubber knife coming at me across a spacious judo mat. It was an enraged stranger with a real knife and I was virtually trapped in a tiny space by bodies and vehicles. I forgot everything I'd learned in my self-defence classes and prepared to run for it. I shot through a gap between two vans but there was a row of awkwardly-parked cars behind them. I found another gap and shuffled as quickly as I could through it, all the time expecting to feel the blade of that knife in my back at any moment.

Then, once I was out in a more open space, I suddenly felt stupid and ashamed. Despite all my training, I'd lost control and given my attacker the advantage. Not only that, I had momentarily forgotten the bunch of children I'd left behind me with an enraged man with a knife. Admittedly he was bent on attacking me and not them but it had still been the wrong thing to do.

I stopped in the middle of a large space and turned to face my attacker. And suddenly I was calm. I knew exactly what I had to do. The man was just a few yards away but instead of backing-away as he expected me to do, I took a step towards him.

When he was almost within touching distance I held up my hand like a traffic cop and shouted 'Stop'. This wasn't a move I'd practised. I just did it instinctively and with confidence and the man stopped in surprise.

I told him I was a judo expert. (Exaggerating a bit because compared to my teacher I was a novice - but I had been doing it for seven years.) 'If you come at me with the knife I'll put you in hospital.' I said, 'And I don't want to do that.' It sounds a bit melodramatic now but I wasn't bluffing. I knew I couldn't afford to take any chances and I would have to hurt him to make sure he couldn't carry-on.

By now we'd got our audience back – dozens of them but instead of a film it was a live performance. The man had the spotlight at that moment and the audience waited to see what he would do. He thought about it for a moment and then his anger drained from him, his shoulders drooped and he just looked deeply upset.

I actually felt a little sorry for him as he was led away without a struggle by some of the management people and I was later asked if I wanted to press charges. I didn't and I never saw him or the woman again.

Tension drains energy

A more convincing but perhaps less personal example of this theory about attitude comes from the great boxer Muhammad Ali. He sometimes lost his temper in the ring but rarely if ever lost his control. His phrase, 'Float like a butterfly, sting like a bee,' was meant to be amusing but it was also sensible. He glided around the ring completely relaxed and therefore using very little energy. Most of his opponents were using-up valuable energy all the time, without actually achieving anything. They were getting tired just keeping their muscles tense and their minds tense too.

It seems like a paradox but they were loosing energy by keeping energy locked-up inside them. This is a bit like taking a deep breath and then keeping the air inside you. You can't do it for very long before it works against you. To work more efficiently energy needs to flow through your body just as oxygen does and energy flows much better through a body and a mind that's relaxed. And it's not only to do with losing energy. It's also about losing the plot.

A boxer out of control is like a powerful car with the driver asleep at the wheel. And what's true for physical situations is also true for purely verbal ones. Stay relaxed and stay focussed. Focus on what you want to gain – not on winning the argument. As I've already intimated: *There's no point in winning a battle but losing the war.*

What about karma in all this?

I'm sure many of you have heard of Karma. It's an Eastern philosophy which roughly-speaking, states that whatever we get out of life depends on what we've put into it. Or as the modern phrase has it, 'What goes around – comes around.'

I believe there's a lot of truth in this and that reminds me of another well-known positive thinking assertion that goes something like this:

'You attract more bees with a tiny spot of nectar than a barrel full of vinegar.'

Of course you may decide to be awkward and say, 'I don't want to attract bees. I want to attract customers into my very British fish and chip (French fries) shop.' In which case you'd probably be better off going with the vinegar. But the principle remains the same. You act with the best interests of all concerned at heart. As I said earlier that's what positive thinking is all about. And it's also good old-fashioned commonsense.

But is there another side to all this? Is there really a 'magical' element called Karma? I'm sure followers of Eastern religions such as Buddhism are sure there is. The few practising Buddhists I've met have impressed me. I like their unselfish approach to life, their kindness and general lack of greed for material things and their reverence for life in all its forms. But the one thing I find a little hard to take is their belief in reincarnation. The idea that you might come back to earth to learn lessons you've missed this time and also to repay debts that you still owe.

Their notion of karma therefore suggests that you might not see the fruits of your efforts – either good or bad – in this lifetime but have to wait for the next one or the one after that. Maybe they are right but in the words of an old-time comedian, Jimmy Durante', I can't wait that long. I only have two changes of clothes.

I find it challenging enough to deal with one life at a time so I'll be keeping my options open. But I have to be honest and say that there *does* seem to be such a thing as karma – in this lifetime. Oddly I find it quite difficult to give positive examples of karma working in my own life whereas I could cite dozens of negative ones.

For some reason I don't quite understand, the good things that happen to me, don't easily relate to the good deeds I've done, other than in a very general way. I'll give a few example of this:

Does tithing 'work'?

For many years now I have given a certain portion of my earnings to charity. You may have heard of 'tithing', which is a Christian idea of giving at least ten percent of your earnings away. Christian friends who are, perhaps, more committed to their faith than I am, often swear to the fact that no matter how much money they tithe an equal or greater amount always comes back to them – and pretty quickly.

One person I know claims to sometimes get back ten times more than he's given away. He says that on occasions it's been almost *exactly* that increase. For example he said he once gave someone in need the sum of £35 at a time when he didn't have very much himself. Just a few days later, and totally unexpectedly, he received a cheque through the post for £350.

I can't claim to adhere to this idea of tithing completely because, as a writer, my earnings fluctuate wildly and I'm not always sure how much (if anything) I've earned in a particular month. But I always give *something* and it's based loosely on this figure of ten percent. Anyway – the point is that I always seem to have enough for things I *really* want – whatever they might be.

I remember, for instance, my wife Pat and myself taking nine children (our own plus foster-children) to Disneyworld in Florida. We'd booked the holiday when I'd been doing well but as the time to actually go on holiday drew near, the money coming-in dried to a trickle and several large bills needed paying.

For the first time in my life – apart from taking out a mortgage – I needed to borrow money. A close relative came to our aid with an interest free loan. Pat was really concerned and thought it would take us an age to repay it but for some reason I was certain we had nothing to worry about. We went to Florida and had a wonderful time. And sure enough we repaid the loan within weeks.

I am also a very lucky person. I rarely gamble on things like the lottery but find it hard to resist buying raffle tickets in a good cause. The amount of times I buy winning tickets is extraordinary. I sometimes find it embarrassing and especially when it happens to me as a guest speaker at some kind of writers' event (where I am being paid as a speaker or tutor and everyone else has paid to get in.)

I don't like drawing attention to myself by refusing to accept the prize because this can look patronising and if I pretend not to *have* the winning ticket then the prize is sometimes put to one side so nobody gets it. So it's hard to know what to do. At a recent event where I'd been engaged as a speaker I was telling one of the delegates about all this, just as the raffle was about to start, and sure enough, a few seconds later, one of my numbers was first out of the hat.

The person I'd been talking to was so surprised he shouted out, 'Over here. Steve's got it.' And of course everyone turned to look at me with disappointment on their faces. A little flustered I asked for that prize to be raffled again.

And then, not wanting to run any risk of the same thing happening again, I quietly handed the rest of my tickets to the young man who'd shouted out my name. A moment or two later he'd won a prize with one of my tickets. He chose a copy of my other book, the writers guide *Writing TV Scripts,* so I was able to sign it for him.

But as I was saying it's sometimes difficult to link the good things that happen *directly* to any specific actions I've taken. On the other hand it seems much easier to link the bad things that happen to me to the bad actions I've taken. Maybe I just have a well-developed guilt complex and take more notice of my 'punishments' because I've come to expect them. (Or maybe – as I'm sure some people will suggest – I actually punish myself.) I'll give a couple of examples so you can make-up you own mind about it.

Telling lies

Many years ago – before I wanted to be a writer – I thought I might become a cartoonist. Why not? I had a decent sense of humour, I could draw a bit and I had a pencil or two. What else did I need? I did about ten drawings and sent them off to a newspaper. They all came back. I did a few more and the same thing happened again. Then I had a brilliant idea. I prayed to God. This is more or less what I said: 'Dear God I *think* I can do something a bit more creative than being a window-cleaner (which is what I was at that time) but I'm not sure about it. Will you please help me?'

Then I asked God to let me sell just *one* cartoon so that I'd know I was on the right track. And I promised that I would give whatever payment I received to charity. I sent off another ten cartoons and I sold one to the Daily Mirror.

I was delighted and expected to get about two pounds for it (As I said this was a long time ago) but when the cheque came it was for eight guineas. This was almost equal to a whole week's wages for me and I realised that our son Robert (I was still married to my first wife Maureen at the time) needed a new pair of shoes for school and some other stuff too. Maureen reminded me about my promise to give the money to charity.

I thought about it for a while and got back in touch with God. 'Dear God,' I said, 'I've just had another brilliant idea – and I think you're *really* going to like this one. Eight guineas isn't a large sum to a charity but it is to me at the moment so I'll spend it on my son. But now I know I *can* do it I'll send a whole lot more cartoons away – get lots of money and give some of *that* to charity. How does that suit you?'

I'm sure you can guess what's coming. I drew over fifty cartoons after that and didn't sell another one. Some years after that, I actually tried once more (without trying to get God to be my agent) and sold one more. But this time to a trade paper that paid only two pounds fifty. By then I'd lost interest anyway. Would things have been any different if I'd kept my original promise to God?

Maybe not but I have a feeling they *might* have been. I would have worked at the task with more optimism and enthusiasm for a start and I'd have kept at it longer. But after I'd told my 'lie' to God my heart was never really in it. It taught me a valuable lesson. I've tried *never* to break a promise again – not just to God but to anybody and in a way I'm pretty sure that's brought good things into my life.

Another time when I behaved badly and suffered for it started when I got involved in an argument over the phone with a stranger who'd called my house to tell me off about something:

Being too 'proud'

In truth I was in the wrong on this occasion but felt challenged by this man's aggressive attitude and didn't want to back down. He accused me of being unpleasant and insulting to a member of his family. He had a point but I actually liked the other person concerned and thought this man was taking the whole thing too seriously. I lost my patience and said something sarcastic to him.

That made him really angry and he made threats against me. I very sarcastically invited him to carry out his threats if he thought he was man enough. I wasn't taking it too seriously. Not only did the man live several miles away but we'd never even met each other or even seen each other.

I put the phone down thinking that was the last I'd ever hear of the matter. The very next day I was walking through the centre of town when I was passed by the very person I'd insulted. She was with a man I'd never seen before. She nodded and gave a terse 'hello' to me. I replied in a similar fashion and carried on walking.

A few moments later the man who'd been walking with the woman grabbed me from behind. Of course it was the same man who had threatened me over the phone the night before.

It turned out that he'd casually asked the woman who she'd just spoken to and she had told him – unaware of the argument we'd had over the phone. Since there aren't *that* many people called Steve Wetton living in Derby in the UK the man had been pretty sure he'd got the right one.

We both ended-up in need of a visit to the local hospital Emergency unit. He to have to have a couple of stitches in his face and me to have a knucklebone reset and a swollen eye looked at. Bad behaviour really doesn't pay on a commonsense level or a possible Karmic one. (But oddly enough we later ended-up on reasonable speaking terms and I quite liked him.)

A more light-hearted example of me being 'punished' for telling a lie happened quite recently:

The 'white' lie

My wife Pat and I called to see a friend, and someone we weren't expecting to see there opened the door. It was another friend but one who lived many miles away and who we don't see very often. Her face lit-up in a smile and she said, 'Steve. Now we can settle the argument. It's about skiing in Switzerland.'

I was puzzled and said, 'Why do you think I'll know anything about that? I've never been to Switzerland' 'Of course you have,' she said as she ushered us into a room filled with other friends, all waiting eagerly for my answer to whatever the question was, 'Don't you remember? That's why you and Pat couldn't come to our wedding anniversary three years ago. You were skiing in Switzerland.'

I don't very often blush but I did then. Is it possible that a working-class person like me could *ever* forget he'd been skiing in Switzerland – let alone forget it after just three years? Than I had a moment of inspiration. 'Oh I see where you've got it mixed-up,' I said, 'Kranska Gora isn't in Switzerland. It's in the former Yugoslavia.' From somewhere close behind me I heard my wife, Pat, choke on the drink she'd just been handed. She couldn't look me in the face for fear of doing it again for at least an hour afterwards. I *think* I got away with it. (Until they read this book!)

So yes, I do believe that, by and large, we seem to reap what we sow. But whether it's Karma, coincidence or cause and effect. What does it matter if it works? So choose a positive and truthful attitude. What have you got to lose? Which leads me to the next question:

Is 'attitude' really just a matter of choice?

If you're thinking it isn't always easy to change your attitude then you are absolutely right. Some situations cause feelings that can't be cured by a quick fix, an effort of will, or a spoonful of positive thinking. If you've just lost a loved one or suffered a terrible accident or been told by your doctor you have a serious illness or perhaps find yourself in a prison cell for something you didn't do. Then of course you can't just switch off your feelings of despair in an instant. No sensible person would try to tell you otherwise.

My wife Pat is quite fond of (mischievously) telling me I would have made a brilliant doctor. She says I wouldn't have had to study hard and learn about medicines or illnesses I would just have needed to practise the simple phrase, 'For Heaven's sake pull yourself together.' But she doesn't really mean it. (And I never actually use that phrase or take such a bossy attitude!) She just means that I encourage myself, and others to consider the facts of any situation.

And the facts usually go like this: As hard as it might be to change your attitude in really difficult situations it would, almost certainly, be much harder to change your *situation*. In fact, your attitude is sometimes the only thing you *can* change. So it makes perfect sense to do it as soon as possible. (And I'll be talking about this from another angle when I deal with making a fresh start – in a later chapter.)

We all know how important attitude really is. How many of us can point to people who have difficulties to cope with yet manage to remain happy and smiling? A woman I know was born with problems, which necessitate the use of a wheelchair for much of her time.

Yet she leads a very full and useful life. She drives a car, has a wide circle of friends, pursues many hobbies and, amazingly, works as a schoolteacher – not the easiest of jobs for anyone these days – yet one she does very well. I have rarely seen her miserable.

In contrast to this I also know people who *seem* to have everything. They may be super-fit, have pots of money, live a life of pampered luxury and do nothing but complain or even waste their lives completely. They sometimes drink themselves to insensibility or ruin their health by taking so-called 'recreational' drugs. You know this is true. You either know people like this personally or read about them every day in the newspapers. That's the awesome power of attitude. Would anyone dare to say that the life of a super-model or a top-class footballer is more successful than the life of my friend the schoolteacher? I don't think so.

So I suggest that it isn't a good idea to sit around moping and waiting for a miracle to happen out of the blue. You can hope and pray for a miracle of course and that makes perfect sense but you must be prepared to help it along. If *all* you learn from this book is how vitally important a change of attitude can be, in making your life better, I promise you it will have been worth it. Your life *will* improve and that improvement can start right now. Right this minute. What are you waiting for?

Points to note

Step One

Change your attitude

- ❖ Change your attitude and you'll change your life – starting right now!
- ❖ Change your attitude first and your circumstances second
- ❖ It's easier to change your attitude than your circumstances
- ❖ Your circumstances *can* change as if by magic – to suit your new attitude
- ❖ You attract more bees with a spot of nectar than a barrel full of vinegar
- ❖ Focus on the result you want to achieve
- ❖ Don't win a battle – but lose the war
- ❖ After-effects can last a lifetime – so choose 'good' actions
- ❖ Attitude affects performance
- ❖ What goes around does *seem* to come around
- ❖ Telling lies – for your own benefit – doesn't pay
- ❖ Attitude really *is* a matter of choice
- ❖ If life hands you a lemon – make lemonade

3 Accept There *Might* Be a Higher Power

Step Two

I THINK I'VE BEEN LUCKY. I seem to have been born with an inherent belief that there's more to life than we can explain in material or scientific terms. Even as a young child I could feel 'vibes' from other people and animals and felt an invisible connection between us all. As I grew older I learned it was sometimes better not to talk about this sort of thing too much – especially if you were male. People might think you were a bit strange.

Thankfully things are changing in this aspect, which is possibly why (if you're a man) you are reading this book. In my opinion we *are* all connected to each other at a spiritual level *and* connected to some invisible something else that's part of the life force itself. I'm convinced of it.

You don't have to agree with me. You don't have to accept that this strange power definitely exists. But I think you'd be wise to accept the possibility that it *might* because then you won't feel so silly trying out some of the techniques we'll be discussing later.

On the other hand, if you still prefer to believe that things just happen by accident or in response to actions you've taken in terms of pure logic, then that's okay too. You can *still* learn something from the techniques in this book. As I said right at the beginning – you behave better – you get a better result. It can be as simple as that. There might, as many people believe, be no 'magic' involved at all. But isn't that a dull and slightly depressing sort of attitude to take? To think there's no magic in life?

As a tv writer I'm often irritated when tv producers say they are looking for more 'gritty realism' in the scripts they are offered. I suppose we all understand what they mean but why is 'grittiness' any more realistic than say cleanliness or light-heartedness? Is a piece of grit any more 'real' than a snowflake or a sunflower? Why don't producers ever say they are looking for a bit of 'frothy realism'? I'd be happy to oblige and I know plenty of other people who feel the same.

I promise you that 'miracles' do sometimes happen. You may vehemently deny this at the moment but who knows? You *might* consider changing your opinion if you decide to read on but we'll see. So if you're still on board let's move on to:

Keeping an open mind

I've already told you of the happenings surrounding my friend Bryan's death and the effect they had on me. Now I'll mention just two more strange experiences I had as a young man that still make me shudder when I think of them. Both happened before my friend's death. The first when I was working for a time as what used to be called a 'tally' man. That is, a person (man or woman) who was part salesperson and part debt-collector. I travelled around in a little van, visiting customers on a door-to-door basis, to sell them more stuff and to collect their weekly payments for the things they'd already had.

It was one of the few jobs I quite enjoyed because it was so varied and you met such interesting people. (A few who occasionally offered to settle their bills in unusual ways but that's another story.) So here we go:

The near miss

I happened to be running late one particular day (nothing to do with the unusual settling of bills I hasten to add) and was sprinting in and out of houses, jumping into my van, practically doing wheelies as I made screeching three-point turns and looked for short-cuts.

At one particular house near the end of a cul-de-sac I drove right into their driveway so I'd be able to reverse into the street facing back the way I'd come. The privet hedges were very short so I had an excellent view all around. This quiet little street seemed totally deserted as I came out of the house and jumped into the van. I looked over my shoulder and prepared to zoom into the street without any obstructions to worry about. But for some unaccountable reason I found my foot lifting of the accelerator and slamming down on the brakes before I'd moved at all.

I slipped into neutral, checked both wing mirrors and again turned in my seat to look out of the back windows. I could see nothing behind me – the way seemed completely clear. I was wasting valuable time.

But despite what I've said about screeching turns I've always been a very careful driver (especially after Bryan's terrible accident) and had only been hurrying in conditions of perfect safety. Now I didn't feel comfortable. I switched off the engine, got out and walked to the rear of my van.

Sitting, very quietly, on the driveway, just inches from my rear bumper, was a little girl – just a toddler. She was happily playing with a toy and completely oblivious of any danger. It transpired that she had 'escaped' from a nearby garden and had no realisation of the dreadfully dangerous position she'd put herself in. She smiled up at me as I gently coaxed her back to her own house.

Now I know what sceptics will say – that I had probably seen the child playing outside on a previous occasion and realised she might be there again that day – or that I must have caught a glimpse of her without fully realising it – or that I'd heard the toy scraping on the ground. And maybe they have a point?

Maybe *something* like that happened. But that's not the way I remember it. I was in an area that wasn't all that familiar to me. To the best of my knowledge I'd never seen the child before and it would have been hard to hear anything less than a shout over the sound of my engine. As far as I'm concerned I just had a 'feeling' that seemed to come from nowhere. I dread to think how I could have lived with the guilt, of what might so easily have happened that day, if I hadn't 'listened' to my inner signals. The second incident of a similar nature probably saved my own life and the life of a workmate. It went like this:

The 'safe' hide-out

The two of us, myself and another labourer, were working at the old Derby Power Station (in the English Midlands) and had been given a particular task to perform by lunchtime. We managed to finish early and were killing time as we waited to go for our break.

We wandered into a part of the site we didn't know very well and found a furnace door to one of the boilers wide open. The door didn't reach down to the floor it was quite small and about three feet off the ground. It was made of thick metal but also lined with fire-proof bricks.

Looking inside the boiler we could see piles of old ashes on the floor and water pipes stretching up the walls like the pipes of a huge church organ. Everything looked rusty and old. We decided it must be a disused boiler and maybe one that was due to be repaired. It looked very interesting.

Incredible as it now seems, we decided to scramble inside and have a closer look. Once inside we stood amongst the cold ashes that seemed like friendly sand-dunes and looked upwards at the lights streaming through small viewing windows' set at least one floor above. The sounds of the factory had disappeared completely. The walls were so thick that even loud noises couldn't penetrate. It was strangely peaceful and relaxing.

My workmate suggested this was the perfect place for us to 'hide' from our bosses for a while. Realising we might be spotted through the open furnace door we managed to pull it into an almost closed position. Then we sat on the ashes and shared a newspaper my workmate had been carrying around in his haversack. He sorted out a little bag of sandwiches and offered me one. It was like a beach picnic but with restricted views and no swimmers.

We stayed like that for about fifteen minutes before I started to feel uncomfortable. With the 'organ' pipes and the quietness I had initially thought it was almost like sitting in the first few pews of a church but now it seemed more like being inside a tomb. I suddenly 'knew' that we shouldn't stay there a moment longer.

My workmate started to argue about it – saying we only had another fifteen minutes to go and we didn't want to be seen standing around doing nothing. He said we'd be given some meaningless task to do *and* expected to do more in future. I refused to listen. I was feeling really worried by then. I lay on my back, pushed the heavy door open with my feet and slid out. I urged my workmate to follow. A bit reluctantly he did. 'You work too hard and too fast,' he said, 'No wonder the other blokes don't like being paired-off with you.'

There was some truth in what he said. I was in my twenties – very fit and strong and I enjoyed a challenge. We'd filled a huge lorry with rubbish in half the time some of the older labourers would have taken and in a way it was a bit unfair that we'd be more likely to be 'punished' for it than congratulated. Our foreman wasn't a bad person because he understood how hard physical work can be but there were people above him who weren't always so considerate.

Anyway we'd been out of the boiler for less than a minute – and still dusting the dry ashes from our overalls when a man in a white boiler-suit came along and closed the furnace door we'd just climbed out of. He didn't just close it – he made sure it was firmly latched into place and then started to walk briskly away towards a staircase leading upwards. I shared a silent look with my workmate. We didn't need to say a word. We each knew exactly what the other was thinking. Had we still been inside the boiler would we have heard anything at all before the door had been closed that final inch or so? And if not would this man have heard us shouting? It seemed unlikely.

The man was very brisk and businesslike and hadn't even noticed us standing there in the open. He'd passed us with barely a glance in our direction. It's true we'd moved away from the furnace door but not that far away. He might have paused to wonder what we were doing there, partly smothered in ashes.

I hurried after the man in the white boiler-suit and politely asked him what was going on. 'Nothing unusual,' he said, 'I'm just starting-up this boiler.' He was a nice man and very interested in his job. He didn't ask us why we were doing nothing. He invited us to go upstairs to the control panel and watch what happened next.

We peered through one of the viewing panels as he pressed a button that released a thick cloud of what looked like black smoke. He explained that it was pulverised coal. He allowed me to press another button. That released a flame and possibly some kind of volatile vapour. The fuel erupted into a huge ball of fire that rolled, red and white, like a vision of hell. It was quite a sight. I realised that from this high position and at this angle we couldn't have seen the floor of the boiler even without the coal-dust and the flames. I politely asked the nice man why he hadn't bothered to look inside the boiler before he'd closed the furnace door.

'What for?' he asked. 'Do you look inside your central heating boiler at home before you turn it on?' Ignoring the fact that I didn't actually *have* a central heating boiler at that time (since my first wife and I lived in a tiny caravan – which I usually described as a detached residence set in rural surroundings) I told him a domestic boiler wasn't likely to have workmen inside it.

'Nor is this one,' he explained, 'Not without my knowledge and the permission of the top management and not without somebody erecting warning signs and sectioning the whole area off with reflective tape. Boilers are very dangerous things you know,' Then he added, 'You have to treat them with respect.'

'Right,' I said, 'So you knew there'd be nobody in there *working* – but supposing somebody was in there for another reason?' 'Such as?' he asked. I was about to say, 'To read a newspaper and eat their sandwiches,' but thought I'd better not. 'Well – just to have a closer look, out of curiosity,' I said. He held my glance for a few seconds as if he'd realised what I was implying but then he dismissed it and smiled, 'What kind of an idiot would do that?' he said.

My workmate and I realised that in all probability, if we'd stayed inside that death trap for just another minute or so we would both have disappeared from the face of the earth without a trace. Even our bones would have been nothing but fine ashes and nobody would have gone looking for them anyway. What reason would they have had to do that? It would have been clear that we'd clocked-in for work that morning, finished one task and then just vanished.

The only thing that sometime gets a laugh when I tell people this story is the thought that my first wife, my son, and all my relations might have thought I'd run off with another man or been abducted by aliens. But joking aside – not a very happy prospect for them or the partner of my workmate – who would all have suffered for years, maybe for the rest of their lives, hoping vainly for us to get in touch.

Very occasionally I've dreamed of what those last few moments might have been like, with that thick metal and brick door being closed completely and the cloud of choking black coal-dust swirling down on us before the explosion of heat and flame hit. If I hadn't, once again, paid attention to my inner 'feelings'.

But was it just my imagination?

I realise that every example of receiving messages I've given so far in this book, has involved myself as receiver of the message. And I've already admitted I might have been fooling myself, so maybe it's time I included a story where someone else plays the main part.

This happened much later, after I'd changed my life around. I was sitting with a group of people who were attending a writers' event at The Hayes Conference Centre in Swanwick, near Derby.

I'd gone to see a friend of mine who was there as a delegate. We met in a pub just outside the conference centre. My friend introduced me to several people and we smiled, shook hands and swapped the usual pleasantries. But one lady, Marian Hough, held on to my hand a moment longer than the others, looked steadily into my eyes and said, 'You look very sad. Is everything alright?'

I told her in no more than a couple of sentences, that several difficult things had happened very recently, including the sudden and totally unexpected death of a close family member. She apologised for being so personal and I told her not to worry. I wasn't upset or offended. The conversation took a more general turn and we all started talking about writing and the courses on offer at the conference.

But during a lull Marion leaned closer to me and whispered, 'Please forgive me for asking but who's John?' Then before I had chance to answer she added, 'And what's cricket got to do with anything? He's standing just behind you and showing me a cricket bat.'

I didn't need to turn around and look for a real live person, with a name- tag, wearing a blazer and carrying some sporting equipment. It was obvious that Marion was looking at somebody that nobody else in the room could see. And the close family member who'd died so recently was my brother John.

Until John had died I'd had three brothers. The other two, like me, were mad about football. John had always been mad about cricket. We'd play for hours in the backyard with a 'real' cricket bat and a tennis ball. Very few people in that working-class district had even seen a real cricket bat but John had a bat of his own. None of the family could bowl him out for what seemed like ages and when anyone did he'd bowl them out within minutes.

He'd had trials for Derbyshire as a youth and later followed them all over the country as a spectator. I can't think of any symbol more appropriate, than a cricket bat, to convince me this lady knew what she was talking about.

In any case she then went on to tell me a couple of things that it would have been almost impossible for her to guess at. Things about the circumstances of John's death. She wasn't just 'fishing' for details and in fact I barely said a word.

She was at pains to tell me something she felt was important, though she didn't understand why. It *was* important – very important. There had been some confusion surrounding John's death and one member of our family was thinking of making a formal complaint against the hospital on the grounds of negligence.

Marion seemed to have some inkling of this and said that John wanted us all to know that his death wasn't the result of an accident. He said we should stop worrying and accept what had happened. He also said he was happy where he was.

To me, this has remarkable echoes with what happened after the terrible accident involving my best friend Bryan and his family – when the bird appeared and seemed to give me a message. Except this time I couldn't have been imagining it because someone else was telling it to me.

Sceptics may claim that I'd told Marian some of these details but as I've already said, I'd barely spoken. She wasn't asking me questions – she was telling me things. And I had just met her for the very first time. So maybe people will say she was reading my thoughts? But if that's true doesn't it tend to prove what I've already said about psychic connections? Which brings me to my next point:

Could thoughts be 'things'?

If my thoughts were floating about in the atmosphere, for anyone to read who had the ability, isn't it just possible that thoughts aren't necessarily extinguished by the death of the person who 'transmitted' them?

I don't see why we should have any difficulty believing that it *might* be possible – and even perhaps *normal* – for us to receive invisible messages without even knowing where they come from. We turn on the television set at the touch of a button on our remote control. We don't see or hear the beam that causes this to work and we certainly don't see pictures floating through the air before they appear on the screen.

The human brain is far more complicated than a tv set. So why should we think it only responds to things that scientists can measure and understand? Can they measure love, sadness or happiness? No. They can only observe the effects these things have on our bodies and our behaviour. Would a scientist say that love doesn't exist because you can't weigh it or measure it?

Are we all connected by a 'universal' energy force?

It won't surprise you to hear that I make no claims to be either a scientist or an intellectual. So I hope you'll bear with me if I try, in my own clumsy way to explain how I sometimes 'see' all humans being connected to each other.

Imagine' if you will, going down to a beach and filling a bottle with water from the sea. If you then take the bottle away from the sea is it still part of the sea or is it something else? It's certainly lost its awesome power until it's returned to its source. Now imagine a human being who might be nothing more than a tiny portion of energy enclosed in a body.

Removed from the 'sea' of universal energy, perhaps he or she becomes, like the sea-water in the bottle, much less powerful – until that person's body dies and their energy returns to the universal energy source.

But there's a difference between these two examples. A human being isn't *entirely* trapped inside his or her body in the same way that water can be trapped inside a bottle. A human being has a mind that just might be able to reach out and contact other minds. Perhaps contact the source of universal energy itself. And how powerful might that be?

Going with the flow

To carry-on a little further using water as a metaphor, can you imagine life flowing like a river? Obviously a river flows more smoothly without dams and boulders being put in its way. Surely your life is just like that. It flows along better without having too many obstacles put in the way. And do you think you might be creating some of those obstacles for yourself? Canoeing on a river can be great fun. I tried it once in America. But it was much easier going downstream than upstream – going with the flow and not against it.

It's true that, as human beings, we sometimes feel that the flow is going in the 'wrong' direction and we feel morally obliged to go against it. But to fight against the current when it's heading in the right direction, as so many people do, just doesn't make sense to me. Or am I just fooling myself again?

What about organised religion?

I happen to be a practising Christian who attends church regularly but significantly the church I belong to is very open-minded and tolerant. If it wasn't I would stop going there. We don't deny people of other religions the right to worship in their own way and anyone is welcomed into our services – whatever their faith.

During a recent radio interview I said I was thinking of writing a book called, *Forget Religion And Start Believing In God.* I was joking but the more I thought about it afterwards the more it seemed like a reasonable idea.

There are so many things I am still doubtful about where organised religion is concerned. I don't like the fact that many religions are so male-biased for a start, or that people of differing religions (or sometimes people of different branches of the *same* religion) want to kill each other. I simply don't understand this.

My own belief is that you don't need to formally worship a God you can distinguish from other Gods and you don't, necessarily, have to follow rigid, man-made, rules you might not agree with. But, on the other hand, my experiences suggest to me that being willing to believe there *might* be a superior power – a power that provides direction and order in the universe – is not only helpful but also commonsense.

Can a human being really think there are no 'natural' rules governing what happens in any way – that every happening is a random event – and there's no sense or pattern to anything?

This reminds me of a nice little story I've heard in more than one, slightly differing version. I'm not sure if it's actually based on something that really happened but it could be and it certainly does get the point across.

The version I give here is based on something I read in an excellent magazine called, *The Word For Today* which is distributed by the Evangelical Christian organisation, United Christian Broadcasting.

Creation or random happening?

A scientist who didn't believe in any kind of God was visiting a friend who happened to be a Christian. These two had discussed the issue of creation many times. The Christian believed that God had made the Universe and given it some kind of Divine order. The scientist thought there was no 'intelligence' at work here. That everything in the universe and on Earth had simply 'happened' at random.

The scientist noticed a little model of a garage made out of Lego blocks and asked if his host's young daughter had made it. The Christian smiled and said, 'Nobody made it. It just 'happened'.

Can you see the irony here? Could even a model made out of plastic blocks just 'happen?' Could the pieces tumble out of a box and assemble themselves in perfect order? Similarly, could the pieces of something much more complicated, like a thousand piece jigsaw puzzle simply form themselves into a perfect picture without any help at all?

So we think it's perfectly sensible to say that a simple Lego model or a jigsaw puzzle has to be *created* by someone. But that amazingly complicated things like, plants, fishes, animals, birds, insects and human-beings can just happen by themselves. Does that really seem sensible?

I began this chapter by asking if a belief in a higher power was necessary. I hope I've made it very clear by now that it can certainly help. But it does no harm to have a questioning attitude. That's the way to learn things. All I'm asking you to do is accept the possibility that there *might* be something beyond human understanding in the universe. Some power, that can come to your aid if you're willing to listen and give the existence of that power the benefit of the doubt.

It's true that it doesn't *always* seem to work but that's no reason to say it doesn't exist or that it might not be working to your advantage in some way that isn't immediately obvious. People, like doctors, teachers, and solicitors, who help us make important decisions in our lives aren't always right but that doesn't mean they don't really exist!

And isn't it a bit silly to say you don't believe in a higher power because you wish for some things that never come true? When you were a child your parents may have seemed like all-knowing, all-powerful beings but they couldn't (and hopefully *didn't*) give you everything you asked for. When they said No you didn't stop believing in their existence. And I'm guessing it didn't stop you asking for other things either. So if you're not yet prepared to believe – just be willing to suspend your disbelief and never stop asking.

Points to note

Step Two

Accept there *might* be a higher power

- ❖ Keep an open mind – you have nothing to lose and everything to gain
- ❖ Why does 'reality' always have to be 'gritty'?
- ❖ Is a speck of grit any more real than a snowflake or a sunflower?
- ❖ Pay attention to your inner-feelings when they are urging 'good' actions
- ❖ Consider the proposition that thoughts may be 'things'
- ❖ If thoughts *are* things then other people may be able to receive them
- ❖ Consider that we all came from the same source of energy
- ❖ Do we always stay in contact with that universal energy force?
- ❖ Don't put obstacles in your own way
- ❖ It's easier to flow downstream than fight against the current
- ❖ It's sensible to go with the flow when it's heading in the 'right' direction
- ❖ Worship a God – not a religion
- ❖ If a toy garage needs a creator could a whole universe just happen?

4 **Set Your Goals**

Step Three

Deciding what you want

IMAGINE GOING INTO A TRAVEL AGENCY and saying you'd love to go on a trip but are not sure *where* you want to go, *when* you want to go or *how much* you're willing to pay. Maybe you'd get lucky and the person talking to you would have lots of time and patience and be willing to help. But sooner or later *you* would have to make the decisions yourself. And think how much easier and quicker this procedure would be if you'd done a bit of thinking in advance.

Now apply this to your life as a whole. Suppose for a moment there *is* a higher power? Some form of Divine intelligence, willing and able to grant some, if not all of your wishes. Would you really want to make things as difficult as possible?

And even if you *don't* believe doesn't it still make sense to choose happiness rather than misery; to look forward to things that you might achieve rather than simply carry-on accepting all the things you don't really want?

More than one book on positive thinking that I read in the early days advised me to start by making a wish list of some of the things I'd love to own or some of the experiences I'd love to have.

It was made clear that I wasn't being asked to limit myself to things that were already within my grasp (if only I could be bothered to make the effort). I was to ask for *anything* that wasn't totally impossible. That is, I could ask for a Rolls Royce car or my own private aeroplane but not the ability to walk on water or teach a goldfish to play a piano accordion.

Anyway, I can't even remember all the things I wrote the very first time I tried it but I certainly do remember some of the ones I chose to include in my list once I started taking it seriously. Here they are:

- I travel to America
- I re-visit Singapore
- I have a job I love and look forward to going to work every day
- I meet another wonderful woman and fall in love again
- We have a family together
- We buy a big house in a really nice area
- I earn £50,000 in a single year
- I write my own tv series

Now you may be thinking that, with the exception of the bits about having my own tv series, and earning £50,000 in a single year, this list isn't all that remarkable or ambitious. I suppose that would be true for many people nowadays but I made this list nearly forty years ago when things were very different. Let's take a brief look at each one of my selections.

Long-haul travel was mainly for well-off people. I came from a very working-class area of Derby, which, as you may know is in the middle of England. Many of my childhood friends hadn't even seen the sea until they were almost grown-up.

And after just losing my latest job, and having no savings at all, a holiday in Skegness, less than a hundred miles away, would have been beyond me. So the idea of travelling to America and Singapore was obviously ludicrous.

As for having a job I loved – well, I'd already tried over thirty jobs and hated nearly every one. Even the 'better' ones I found only bearable. I had no formal qualifications at all and a very poor track record. The thought of having a job I loved seemed almost as impossible as the wishes involving walking on water and having a goldfish that could busk.

Meeting another wonderful woman wasn't impossible. Derby's always had its fair share of those. But finding one who might want to start a family with *me* was a very different matter. I was (and unfortunately still am) a short, stocky and very ordinary looking man. I was unemployed (if not unemployable) penniless, jobless, lacking in ambition or qualifications and on top of all that I'd just been divorced for cruelty. Hardly a great catch. It's hard to see how I'd ever attracted my first wife.

Buying houses at all was a rarity for working-class people in those days – never mind buying a big house in a really nice area. The house

I'd be thrown out of after my divorce was owned by the council and my first wife and I been paying rent.

As for earning £50,000 in a single year, well, up to that point in my life I had never earned more than about £1,250 in a single year. Was it likely that I'd one day earn *forty* times more than that? Even if you are getting a lower than average wage at this moment, multiply it by forty, and you'll get some idea how ambitious my wish must have seemed to me when I first wrote it down. I more or less plucked that figure out of thin air and didn't take it very seriously myself.

And finally I had never written a drama script of any kind and didn't even know what a tv script looked like. I had written perhaps half a dozen short stories and managed to sell just one of them. Could I *really* go from that tiny success to having my own series on national television?

Looked at in this light, everything on my list would surely have seemed laughable to anyone who knew me at the time. Yet, incredibly, every one of these wishes came true.

I travelled to America and to Singapore, as well as to various other countries. I became a schoolteacher and enjoyed it so much that I really did look forward to Mondays! I did meet and marry another wonderful woman and did have a family – with as many as nine children at one point – hers, ours and other people's. (We became foster-parents.) Then we *needed* to buy a bigger house and when we did it turned out to be one in a very nice area.

And though it was hard work having such a large family (for my second wife Pat much more than me) it was great fun and very fulfilling. It also didn't stop me from writing a successful tv series. In fact my series just happened to be a comedy drama about the lives of a married couple who decide to become foster-parents. How this came about was really quite strange.

How I became a scriptwriter

I was in the office of a radio producer at the BBC and 'pitching' ideas to him. Naturally I'd started off with what I thought was my best idea. It was the one I'd already written as a complete script and the one that had got me inside his office in the first place but he didn't want to pursue it any further.

I moved on to what I thought was my second-best idea and he didn't like that one at all. By the time I'd reached my sixth idea I was practically making things up on the spot and he was still shaking his head.

Finally I had to admit I had nothing else to talk about. I quietly accepted that I'd probably blown my big chance. I put my script and outlines back into my shoulder bag and prepared to leave.

'I do like your writing,' the man said, 'Your characters and your dialogue in particular, but none of your ideas really grab me.' Then as I was going out of the door he said, 'Don't give up. I'll be happy to look at anything else you send.'

By then I didn't really want to talk anymore. I wanted to punch him for wasting my time and money. The fare to London had been more than I'd expected and I'd had to get-up at dawn to catch the train and I was feeling just the tiniest bit fed-up. But this was the *new* me – the positive thinking me.

I gritted my teeth and managed to say, 'I appreciate your encouragement but I have a full-time job as a teacher and a big family including foster-children and I need to sleep and eat occasionally and go to the toilet so...' and then I started out of the door, feeling just a bit sorry for myself, and convinced I'd never see the inside of this building again.

But the man stopped me. 'Hang on,' he said, '*That* sounds interesting,' 'Which bit?' I asked. 'All of it,' he said, 'A person who's teaching and trying to write but still has time to become a foster-parent. That was a really brave decision. Come back and tell me all about it.'

Incredibly this chance remark that I'd made led to me writing a 30-minute comedy drama series for radio called *Growing Pains*. And later on I turned this same idea into a 50-minute series, with the same name, for television. As I've already said it was all about a couple who become foster-parents. We did twelve episodes for radio and twenty for television. So was there Karma happening here or was it just a logical cause and effect sequence? I'll leave you to decide.

Earning good money

And here's an interesting point: in the year that I wrote ten of those tv episodes I was paid almost exactly £50,000. Which brings me back rather neatly to the subject of how your goals are worded. (And I'll be dealing with this in more detail very shortly.) Instead of writing, 'I earn £50,000 in a single year' perhaps I should have written, 'I earn at least £50,000 every year for the rest of my life'?

I'm only joking here because I've never really been that interested in money and sometimes think it causes more problems than it solves. And my level of happiness hasn't always had much to do with the amount of money I've had at any given time. But it is a little curious that things worked out like that.

And just in case £50,000 a year doesn't seem impressive by the time you are reading this book I can remember thinking at the time it was much more than my hard-working father and most of his friends had managed to earn in a whole lifetime.

This included people who often toiled for five or six days a week from dawn till dusk, on building-sites and down coalmines, with maybe two weeks holiday a year. I'd earned it by doing something I loved and might well have done for nothing.

Ever since I started believing in the power of positive thinking I've had a wonderful life (And please note that I *didn't* really believe in it at first – I was just prepared to give it a try.) I hope you'll do the same and that you'll eventually feel – about your own life – the way I now feel about mine. I really mean it.

But let me make it clear once again that none of these good things happened overnight and some took several years to achieve. But, as I've said, eventually, every single one of them did come true.

Not only that – I didn't have to wait a single day to start reaping the benefits. The very moment I decided to start believing my dreams might come true was the moment my life changed for the better. *I wasn't just focussing on the destination I was enjoying the journey* That's possibly the greatest lesson I learned in all of this:

Where do you make a start?

With hindsight, I now realise, that being at rock bottom and having nothing to lose might have been an advantage to me. I had no way to go but up. This might be the case for you too. But you don't *have* to do things the hard way. Wouldn't it make more sense to start from wherever you are right now (assuming you're not at rock bottom) and learn from my mistakes as well as your own?

I promise you that following these procedures wasn't that difficult for me. I wasn't suddenly working harder I was learning how to work *smarter* by focussing on things I enjoyed and moving away from things I hated. I was just making better choices. *And if an idiot like me (I mean like I was) can do it – anybody can.* Trust me on that. I know what I'm talking about. Would you climb inside a boiler to eat a sandwich and read a newspaper? Well there you are then.

How to start your own wish-list

Let's have some fun with this. Grab a pen and something to write on and in a very short while I want you to start brainstorming (on your own) for ten minutes or so. In a short while I'm going to suggest you write down all the things, happenings and situations, you can think of that would make your life more exciting, more joyful and more fulfilling.

Don't waste time thinking about it *before* you start and don't worry if the things you write seem silly or *almost* impossible. Enjoy the silliness of it all. Remember how you felt as a child, when you could be scoring a goal for your country in your own back yard or dancing on a cloud in your bedroom.

Nobody thought you were crazy or wasting your time back then because, in a way, you were rehearsing for your life as a grown-up and sensible people realised that. Now you'll be preparing for your new life as a more fulfilled grown-up. (And this time nobody will even know about it unless you tell them!)

We'll be looking a bit more critically at what you write very soon. But please understand I'm talking about 'things' you can possess or experiences you can have. I'm not talking about developing aspects of your own personality or your physical fitness – directly. These two tasks will be included in a second list I'll talk about later.

So what kind of things have you always dreamed of owning and what kind of things have you always dreamed of doing? Why not put this book aside for ten minutes or so and write down whatever comes into your head. Why not do it now?

And if you tried that little task – welcome back. Let's move on:

Getting a sensible balance

Before you start refining your own list you might care to have another look at my own. You'll see that it's varied. I didn't simply gone for a list of 'things' I'd like to own. And money came way down on it. I've always been more interested in people than things anyway and I think that shows. There's no reason for your list to be in any way similar to mine but I think it can be useful to categorise things. That way you're more likely to achieve a sensible balance to your ambitions. And I think it's pretty obvious *the universe loves balance*. You could categorise what I've written something like this:

Travel and adventure
Career development
Personal relationships
Living accommodation
Money
Creative ambitions

You might like to use this as a checklist with regard to you own wishes and you might also want to add categories of your own. Perhaps something to do with possessions: a new car, a yacht, an indoor swimming pool, your own racehorse or whatever takes your fancy. That's all stuff we might classify as your 'outer' wants.

In a little while we're going to consider making that second list I mentioned a few moments ago. That list will be more about what we might call your 'inner' wants. (Or more truly your inner *needs*.)

Those aspects of personality and physical fitness you might need to improve to become more the person you really want to be. Remember what's been said about changing your attitude before changing your circumstances? And your attitude doesn't just effect your personality – it has a great impact on your health and fitness too.

The important thing for now is to concentrate on this first list and whittle your selection down to ten at the most. I've always preferred to have anything between six and ten items at a time. Of course you'll be able to add, subtract or revise your list at any time. And I'd advise you to look at your list at least once a month to see if it needs revising anyway.

Meanwhile – don't wait till you have perfect understanding of this technique – just give it a try and learn by experience. If you follow the next few pieces of advice you may find you've eliminated a few more of your wishes. That doesn't matter. Just go back to your brainstorming and find a few replacements.

Maybe, you're getting into the swing of it by now and will go for more ambitious goals this time? To paraphrase an old saying: '*Reach for the stars and you might reach the moon – reach for the kerb-side and you could end up in the gutter.*' Don't limit yourself too much. Relax and have fun. But be sensible too:..

Ensure you have compatible wishes

Check to see that *all* your wishes are compatible with each other and you haven't made one wish that could cancel another wish out. It might not be a good idea to write, 'I train to be a ballerina with the finest ballet company in Europe' but also, 'I am a world champion sumo wrestler' or 'I run my own sheep farm in New Zealand.'

I think you can probably see why – but I could be wrong on this. It's a weird and wonderful world we live in and maybe somebody really *has* done all three of those things successfully? Maybe they created a new form of ballet for larger people and sumo wrestling takes place all over the world nowadays and they could have appointed an under-manager to run the sheep farm in New Zealand whilst they kept in touch via the internet.

But maybe something a bit less daunting might be more appropriate for your very first list! As always it's your decision!

Don't have self-defeating wishes

Similarly it might prove awkward if you only think of yourself and include things that are going to affect your loved ones in ways that could make life really difficult for all concerned. If you are dying to live in an igloo in Greenland make sure your partner and children aren't currently taking scuba-diving lessons and searching the Internet for properties in Barbados.

I'm exaggerating to make a point but this is no small matter. It *really* is vital you get off to a good start. We are talking about your life journey here and unless you want to travel solo you need to choose a destination that other people are as excited about as you are.

(Okay – *nearly* as excited will probably be okay. But dead-set against is a definite No-no!)

Keep things positive

Only include things you *want*. Don't write about things you want to get rid of. So don't put things like, 'I hate this house and would like to move out of it.' If you do that then your subconscious mind may dwell on the most powerful word in that sentence – which is 'hate'. And you could very easily find yourself feeling more of that! So to keep it positive you might say, 'We live in a lovely new bungalow in a quiet area near a park,' or whatever.

Your subconscious mind seems to deal better with straightforward concepts than tricky bits of grammar so don't write convoluted sentences like, 'I'm fed-up going to the same place every year for a one week holiday on a camping site. I want to travel further and do something more adventurous.' Just write something short and to the point like, 'I go on a round the world cruise on a luxury liner,' or 'I fly to Peru and climb Macchu Pichu.'

Use these 'rules' to apply to all your wishes. And *never* include wishes that call for bad things to happen to other people. This is a positive wish-list. Not an attempt at black magic. (Which I've found to be a very dangerous pastime to yourself as well as others. Please don't laugh at this and dismiss me as a crank. I could give some pretty convincing examples of this but that might take another book!).

Wording is important

Keep your wording of things in your list brief and generally in the present tense. So don't write, 'I intend to visit America (or Europe) one day if I can ever afford it' but write boldly and unequivocally, 'I visit America.', or ' I visit Europe.'

Brief or detailed (It's your choice)

Some books on positive thinking advise you to add more details to your affirmations, so instead of specifying America as a destination you might say 'New York', or instead of Europe you might say 'London' or 'Paris' and also give the name of a top hotel there or even a particular suite in that hotel and say what you have for breakfast each day.

I have no quarrel with this. I know it works because I have friends who've done it that way. But this book is about how positive thinking worked for *me* and I'm a lazy sort of person in some ways. Also I like surprises and think by being too specific you might be limiting your chances and slowing their delivery down rather than simply making your request more clear.

You'll see, for instance, that I didn't write of going to America on *holiday*. I actually wrote of *visiting* the country. I can't remember doing this intentionally – it was just a happy accident because instead of paying to go on holiday I got a free return flight and was paid to work there for several weeks in a summer camp. It was in a beautiful mountain region not all that far from New York.

I also hitch-hiked all over the country on my own, walking and being driven, through maybe twenty states in the process. I travelled about a thousand miles in the back of a garbage truck with the side panels open – giving a panoramic view of the countryside and travelling at about forty miles an hour. (It was a brand new truck that was being delivered I hasten to add – not one actually doing its job). I even stayed a few nights at the home of the truck-driver, in Tucson Arizona, and met his wife and children. They were incredibly kind and welcoming to me, a complete stranger.

And then one night, as I moved even further west, I fell asleep on someone's lawn. In the morning I was woken-up by a tough-looking man in a cowboy outfit (but a real one), pointing a six-gun at my chest. I had the presence of mind to say, 'I don't remember asking for an early call,' and giving him what I hoped was a friendly smile. After I'd told him who I was and explained what I was doing there (trying to get to the Grand Canyon for free) he invited me inside his large house for breakfast.

This was served to me by a very attractive and scantily clad young lady who seemed to have half a dozen sisters of exactly the same age and with a very similar dress sense. I realised it wasn't an ordinary house at all but a place of business and the girls had just finished a night-shift. They fed me and gave me coffee and asked for nothing in return. I was invited to use the bathroom to freshen-up and to have a swim in the outdoor pool.

Later on the tough-looking man drove me to a place on the highway where he thought I had a better chance of getting another lift. He waved as he drove off and said, 'Have a nice day.' It seemed incredible. It wasn't just the nice, ordinary people who were being kind to me – even the tough-guys were joining-in. But just imagine if I'd tried to put all *those* kind of details into my wish-list!

Okay, there's just a chance that travelling across a country in the back of a garbage truck or falling asleep outside a certain kind of business establishment (however friendly the occupants might prove to be) isn't the kind of experience you'll be looking for (there's no accounting for taste!).

But I'd always dreamed of going to America and as a child I was really 'hooked' on western films and later 'road' movies. So my wish-list worked in a spectacular way for *me* just as it's worked for plenty of others and that's the important thing.

Time-scale

Many self-help books advise you to make your list more effective by setting yourselves various time limits. They might tell you to write separate lists for the targets you intend to achieve in say, one year, three years or ten years. I can see the sense in this and if it suits you then by all means give it a try.

But I've never been able to do it. As I've already said I don't like to have my life planned out in too much detail. But also I think I'd start worrying as a deadline got closer and I'd find myself focussing on the problems rather than the goals.

It's true that I eventually gave myself a deadline for the writing of this book and I *did* find that helpful. But that was different because it was mostly down to my own efforts and that's something I could, more or less, directly control. If, on the other hand, your wishes are about being offered a particular job, or meeting someone who will prove to be enormously helpful to you then these are things you can't *directly* control.

I can see myself getting very frustrated indeed by trying – not only to make amazing things happen – but by trying to make them happen *on time*. I see no harm in giving myself a kick-up the butt when I need it, but to try and do that to people you haven't even met, seems a bit wrong somehow. And I think it would be terrible to give-up on an ambition because it hadn't happened on schedule.

Why give yourself this extra burden? So include time limits if it suits you but otherwise learn to be more flexible and go with your instincts. And that's it so far with regard to your wish-list involving your 'outer wants'. And in case I've confused you by giving so many details about my own experiences let me give you a reminder of the main points to consider in the making of your list:

1. Don't set your sights too low
2. Whittle items down to ten at the most
3. Keep a sensible balance between them
4. Don't include personality traits or physical well-being (directly) on this list
5. Keep your wishes compatible with family harmony
6. Don't have self-defeating (conflicting) wishes
7. Keep them positive
8. Remember wording is important
9. Brief or detailed (Your choice)
10. Time-scale included or not (Your choice)

And that's it for this list. In the next chapter we'll be looking at that second list I mentioned. The one to do with your 'inner wants' or needs.

Points to note

Step Three

Set your goals

❖ Decide on your destination before you start your journey
❖ But don't just focus on your destination – enjoy the journey
❖ Go for things you really want – not for things already within your grasp
❖ Don't work harder – work smarter
❖ Do things you enjoy – then work becomes play
❖ If you're at rock-bottom the only way to go is up
❖ Why wait? Why not start from wherever you are right now?
❖ Make your own mistakes but learn from mine while you're waiting

❖ If an idiot (like I was) can do it – anybody can. And that includes you.

❖ Use the check-list to finalise your goals

❖ Consider revising your list at least once a month

❖ Don't set your sights too low

❖ Be flexible and you might end-up with something better than you asked for

❖ Remember it's supposed to be fun! So don't stress over it

5 **Prepare Yourself for Success**

Personal qualities

WE'RE NOW GOING TO MAKE THAT second list, this time to do with your general well-being and your 'inner' needs. You won't be brainstorming this time because I think most people find personal qualities much trickier to deal with than simple 'wants'. By and large I think we tend to daydream about the things we'd like to experience or possess rather than improving our own inner qualities.

Physical fitness can be a tricky area because it comes somewhere in between the two. But in general I decided to leave wishes about both physical and mental well-being to this second list. Don't worry about this distinction. I'll have a little more to say about it later in the chapter on self-hypnosis. And you'll be combining the two lists together anyway.

But in the meantime I decided that some specific suggestions for you to consider might be helpful. Here are some I've developed for my own use over the years. I first learned the value of making such a list in a book called: *The Lazy Man's Way To Riches* by Joe Karbo. (updated in 1995 by Richard Gilly Nixon and published by F.P.Publishing Co. Inc, Nevada USA 1-884337-22-8).

You can also find similar suggestions in books going right back to the early pioneers in the subject of positive thinking like Dale Carnegie who I mentioned earlier. In fact the great French psychologist Émile Coué was urging the use of repeated phrases like, 'Every day, in every way, I'm getting better and better' as long ago as the 1920's, to aid self-development.

So where better to start than with a very slight variation on this? Followed by two others in similar style. I'd encourage *everyone* to consider using these first three affirmations but, as always the choice is yours, and I'll leave you to choose from the rest or even make-up some of your own:

- Each day in every way I'm getting better and better.
- I am a friendly and warm-hearted person who attracts other people of a similar nature.
- I am happy and successful. I achieve my goals honestly and without taking advantage of other people.

These are the really vital ones in my opinion. Now here are the rest for you to add to or simply chose from. Just read them all first before starting to make your selection. Some are very personal to myself but I'll be surprised if you can't find others that will suit you – perhaps with a bit of re-phrasing.

- I try to help others without boasting about my good deeds.
- I accept challenge and argument calmly because I know that's how problems are best resolved.
- I face all my problems with courage and enthusiasm and this helps me to deal with them more easily.
- I am able to concentrate fully on any task.
- I feel comfortable in all sorts of situations and with all sorts of people.
- I have confidence in my own abilities. I know I'm capable of great achievements.
- I am honest with myself and therefore with everyone else.
- I am strong and powerful.
- I am very fit and very agile.
- My joints are supple and healthy.
- Energy flows through me. I am filled with energy.
- I am good at seeing creative solutions to any problem.
- I am always calm and cheerful.
- I am a powerful and entertaining speaker.
- I always give generous credit to people who help me knowing that the willing support of others is essential to my own success.
- I see the world as a place of abundance. A place where there is enough for everybody when people care about each other.
- I achieve the best result with the minimum of time and effort.
- I can gently persist in any task without offending others.

- I am well organised in every area of my life.
- I have an excellent memory that gets better every day.
- I read quickly and easily with great comprehension of all the relevant subject matter.
- I feel comfortable showing my emotions honestly.
- If I'm angry I show it in a controlled and reasonable way.
- If I'm happy I want to share my happiness. If I am sad I admit it but then move on.
- I am easily able to relax as deeply as I wish at any time. I use this ability to conserve my creative energy.
- I make decisions quickly.
- The more challenging the problem the more my intelligence is stimulated by tackling it.
- I enjoy meeting new people. I am able to put them at their ease and give them confidence.
- I am loyal to all who depend on me.
- I take pride in a job well done.
- I am prepared to do more than required and 'go the extra mile.' This has a positive effect on all concerned.

I could go on and on. And once again I suggest you select between six and ten of these. Don't overwhelm yourself. If you start with just a few you can always add more later but if you try to hard you may put yourself off completely. As always it's easy does it.

So once you've done this little exercise you should have your two lists ready to use. But how do you use them? That's the next step.

Points to note

Step Four

Prepare yourself for success

- ❖ You need to change yourself to change your circumstances
- ❖ Don't overwhelm yourself by trying to do too much at first
- ❖ Start with a small list and add more things later
- ❖ Add things to your list to suit your own needs
- ❖ And once again it's supposed to be fun

6 **Use Daily Affirmations**

Turning your two lists into one

ONCE YOU'VE INTEGRATED YOUR TWO LISTS into one it will become your **Daily Affirmation List.** I like to mix items from each list rather than keep them as one list following another but I always *start* with a personal development affirmation (or even two or three) because it somehow feels 'right' to do this - more within the spirit of the exercise.

You're probably familiar with the expression 'Life is a matter of give and take', so you'll realise that the 'give' comes before the 'take.' And though you're not actually giving anything away in this instance I think you'll get my point. By wanting yourselves to be a 'better' person you are, in a sense, showing commitment to others.

I've suggested you keep your list small at first – so maybe you'll have a total of twelve or fourteen things on your completed affirmation list. I vary the amount on my own list from time to time but never have more than twenty. I also review them every few weeks and make changes whenever I feel like it. As I've already implied I like to have variety and flexibility in my thinking. Just so long as I'm steadily moving forward in a positive way and enjoying the process.

That matters, to me, much more than stubbornly fixating on specific things and being disappointed if I don't get them. As I've intimated earlier, if I keep an open mind, I may get something even better, than the thing I've been asking for.

Using your daily affirmations list

Once you've sorted out your Daily Affirmations List, write it down, or print it out, in an attractive and easily readable form. I sometimes use different colours for different wishes – like bright red for energy or lilac for calmness and so on. This helps to make the task more enjoyable.

And all being well you are going to be reading it again and again. You should try doing this every day and preferably twice a day. Once in the morning, as soon as you wake-up, and once at night just before you go to sleep.

But don't worry if you can't keep up with this. Once a week – at any time of day – and in black and white is better than nothing at all. Remember this is supposed to be *fun*! It only needs to take a few minutes if you're busy. Just sit quietly and read the list silently or aloud.

Don't skim over it, read every single word, but there's no need to make a big deal out of it either. Don't strain yourself trying to make something happen. You can visualise some of the things you are asking for or 'see' yourself acting in desirable ways if you are good at this sort of thing but I must admit I've always found this difficult to do.

I'm one of those people who usually think in 'words' rather than pictures so I'm more likely to mentally 'rehearse' conversations I'd like to have in certain situations. But if I don't feel like doing that either, I just read the list. And it still seems to work for me.

Don't get anxious about any of it and don't start wondering how on earth some of these things can come about. Just do what I'm suggesting and see what happens. Ideally, your attitude should be – if it happens that's great – if it doesn't what have I lost? I've spent a few minutes relaxing and thinking happy thoughts. What harm can that do?

And don't worry too much about how long you ought to continue doing it before you give-up or before it starts working for you. I'm pretty sure that it's bound to work to some degree for everybody – just as physical training does – but that doesn't mean that everyone who tries it will keep on doing it.

And there's no set time-period involved. People differ in any learning situation so trust your own instincts in the matter. If you enjoy doing it carry on. If not just stop doing it. Oh and there's just one more practicality before we move on:

Don't talk about your list

I was almost going to say, keep your list a secret, from everyone including your partner and close family members in case their (possible) scepticism has a negative effect on you. Or in case they do the opposite and start by being very supportive, until nothing seems to be happening.

At which point their disappointment may put unwanted pressure on you. This is a very real concern. I've already advised you against setting deadlines for yourself so it's not a good idea to let other people do it for you – however unwittingly.

But I also remember how I have, occasionally, left little 'reminders' to myself, scattered about the house. Sometimes these might be drawings I'd made, pictures cut-out of a magazine, or cryptic sentences, written on paper and stuck-on the bathroom mirror or wherever. These reminders were of things I'd decided to particularly concentrate on for a certain period.

At first anyone else living in the house might comment but nobody seemed to notice after a while. So perhaps the best advice is not to *involve* anyone else. Don't be secretive about what you are trying to do but don't go into details either.

So how is it supposed to work?

And once again I can't say for certain. I just know that it can and sometimes does. Maybe it's entirely practical and you are simply focusing more on the things you want to gain. You've set some kind of search mechanism in motion and it forces you to start taking more notice of the things that will help you in your endeavours.

You can do a little experiment to see what I mean by this. All you need to do is think of a colour, then close your eyes and try and visualise all the things in your house and garden with that colour in them. If this is too easy, then include the outside of your neighbours' houses too.

You'll soon realise how many things there are surrounding you that you pay absolutely no attention to at all. Try to visualise garage doors in your neighbourhood and you'll probably give-up after a few moments but have your own garage doors painted and for a while you'll become a garage door expert. Your attention has been drawn to them by self-interest.

And what's true in that particular case must surely be true in a wider sense. If you are telling your subconscious that you want to be slim and healthy – can you be surprised if you suddenly start noticing that 'new' gymnasium that was opened at the end of your road eight years ago? Or maybe it isn't just a practical matter and there really *is* a magical element to all this? Who can say with any certainty? Just give it a try and see what happens.

Add one more twist

So now you've got your Daily Affirmations and you know how to use them so you can heave a sigh of relief. It's like looking at your holiday itinerary even if you haven't yet confirmed the booking.

Just by being hopeful right *now* this very minute you are experiencing happiness rather than misery. Don't knock it. And there's one more thing you can add to this technique. It's something else I read about in Joe Karbo's book as well as in several other books on self-help.

Not only will it help you with the personal qualities on your list but also with that important attitude change we've already talked about. Joe Karbo talked about making 'Super suggestions to your subconscious mind,' and in a book called. *Your Super, Natural Mind* by Sandra McNeil, published by Angus And Robertson in 1981 ISBN 0-207 -95984-6 she writes about, 'Reaching your psychic energy base'. Nothing wrong with either of those two descriptions but I'll call it simple self-hypnosis. And using my version of this tried and trusted technique moves us on to the next step.

Points to note

Step Five

Use daily affirmations

- ❖ If life is a matter of give and take – then remember the 'give' comes before the 'take.'
- ❖ Start you list with a personal development affirmation (or more than one)
- ❖ Again – keep your list small at first
- ❖ Try to read your list every day – but once in a while is better than never at all
- ❖ Use visualisation if you can

❖ But visualisation or not the process still works. I know – it does for me

❖ If it works – great! If it seems not to work – what have you lost? A few minutes a day spent being calm and hopeful?

❖ How long should you continue doing this exercise? Well – how long should you continue exercising at the gym or playing five a side football? That's right. Until you don't want to do it anymore. It's entirely up to you

❖ Don't discuss the finer details of your affirmations list with other people – maintain your own focus

❖ Don't worry about *how* it works. There may be some 'magic' to it or it may be simply cause and effect. What does it really matter?

7 **Use Self-Hypnosis**

Step Six

BEFORE I TELL YOU HOW YOU to use self-hypnosis I want to say a few things about the subconscious mind in general.

How does your subconscious mind work?

This is a trivial happening really but it should serve as a good example because I think it's something we can all relate to in one way or another. I was running goalwards down the middle of a five-a-side soccer pitch and anticipating a pass from the wing. The ball flew towards me low and hard. I'd got clear of my marker and had only the goalkeeper to beat but that wasn't going to be easy. He was young and quick and big enough to cover every inch of the small goal-net.

I shaped to hit the ball first-time with my right foot and sensed, rather than saw, the goalie leaning ever so slightly to his left to block the shot I was about to make. Instinctively I let the ball fly past my right foot and steered it towards the net with the inside of my left foot. The goalie was still going the wrong way and on his knees by now as the ball slid past his heels and into the net. He stood up and shook his head in surprise before saying, 'You jammy old devil..' (or words to that effect) 'How the hell did you *do* that?'

And the answer was, of course, that I didn't *know* how I'd done it. For that split-second my body had seemed to have a mind of its own.

I hadn't directed my thoughts consciously. I couldn't possibly have had time to think, 'He's expecting me to kick the ball with my right foot and he's already moving to his left so I'll let the ball go past me, stick-out my left leg and turn the ball into the other corner.' I just *did* it and it worked beautifully. And I felt elated. I was with nine of my friends, playing a friendly match, inside a school gymnasium but I could practically hear a television commentator shouting (in the same way the commentator had done when England won the World Cup back in 1966) 'They think it's all over – well it is now!'

And haven't we all had moments like that? Maybe yours came while you were dancing, playing badminton, or cricket, or golf, or just catching a fragile ornament as it was hurtling towards the floor. You suddenly realised that some silent part of your brain can make decisions and take actions without taking some kind of vote on them with the full 'committee'. And then you're reminded that we do that kind of thing all the time. We 'allow' our bodies to act on automatic pilot. Life would be very difficult if we didn't.

Imagine walking down the street and having to consciously think of how you are doing it. 'Now swing the left leg and the right arm forwards and turn the head to the right to look for traffic and breath out and keep your heart beating..' and so on.

So it's pretty obvious that much of what we do is not being directly controlled by our conscious thoughts. Which means that it *is* being controlled by thoughts we're not really aware of. And that's a bit scary. Especially if they are not always our own thoughts but sometimes the opinions other people are constantly giving us?

We've all heard of brain-washing but does that only happen to prisoners under torture or can it happen quietly and surreptitiously?

By a nagging partner perhaps or a bullying boss, or even some person we respect and admire who is doing his or her best for us – but getting it wrong or being over-protective? Just how much influence do we allow others to exert over us without being aware of it? Which brings me to the fascinating subject of hypnotism in general:

Hypnotism

I still remember the very first time I saw a stage hypnotist at work. His name was Peter Casson and he was appearing in my home town at the Derby Hippodrome. This was in the 1950's and I was barely in my teens. He was an impressive man to begin with and apparently used his powers to help people in a clinical way as well as being an entertainer. He talked a little about hypnosis then asked the audience to clasp their hands together with fingers interlocked. He then asked us to imagine that our fingers were become more and more tightly stuck together.

I dutifully joined-in but with a part of me holding-back. I suppose I didn't really want to think this stranger could persuade me to do something I might not want to do. So as he was saying 'Your grip is getting tighter,' I was automatically saying to myself, 'Oh no it isn't,' but even then feeling a bit fearful that it *might* be.

I have no way of knowing how everyone else felt. Whether or not they were co-operating more enthusiastically than I was but when Peter said, after just a few seconds, 'Your hands are now so tightly held together that you may not be able to move them apart,' I was astonished to see that at least thirty or forty people sitting around me couldn't separate their hands. They had to walk towards the stage until Peter gave them a gentle tap and told them to relax. Then they did it easily. It was like watching a magician.

Most of these people went back to their seats, once their hands had been released, but about ten of them were asked to go up on stage and become part of the act. Peter was very polite and didn't try to force anyone to do this against his or her wishes. But I assume he was choosing people he thought would make particularly good subjects. The sight of grown men and women standing on that stage, looking sheepish, with their hands locked together, and apparently being powerless to help themselves, was hard to believe.

In fact, if I hadn't recognised several of then as being regular theatre-goers I would probably have concluded that they were all paid stooges just *pretending* to be partially hypnotised. Then Peter Casson really got into his stride and put some of these 'volunteers' into a deeper trance. Soon, one of them, a young soldier in uniform, who I actually knew, was soon trying to open his tunic to 'breast-feed' a doll that he'd been told was crying because it was hungry.

As far as I remember Peter stopped him before it got too embarrassing and gave him a bottle to use instead. Another man was told, that for the rest of this evening inside the theatre, he would immediately fall fast asleep every time he heard the orchestra play a song called 'So Tired'. And he did, even after he'd returned to his seat in the audience believing he was now fully awake and back to normal. It was, to me, an astonishing performance and very good 'evidence' of how powerful suggestions made directly to the subconscious mind can be.

I've described this at length because I genuinely think we tend to dismiss things we might see like this, probably on television these days, as 'trivial' forms of entertainment and then get on with our hectic lives. I want you to think about the implications.

If a total stranger can get a macho young soldier (which I promise you this man definitely was) to think, even for a few minutes, that he was a mother with a baby then just imagine what effect you might be able to have on yourself by talking to your subconscious in a similar way. And doing it – not just on one isolated occasion, but on a fairly regular basis for days, weeks or possibly even months at a time? It isn't that difficult to see the possibilities is it? So how do you actually set about it?

I'll do my best to tell you about that now:

Using self hypnosis

And once again I'm going to remind you that I'm no expert on this. I can only tell you how I do it and as I've already said, I like to keep things nice and easy. First of all choose just one item from your Daily Affirmations list. Commonsense will probably tell you that it has to be a 'personal quality' you want to strengthen or develop – not a 'thing' you're hoping to acquire.

If you hypnotise yourself into becoming calm and friendly and it works then that's fine but if you hypnotise yourself into believing you already have a Rolls Royce in your garage, when you haven't, then you are defeating the object of the exercise.

When you state that you *have* a Rolls Royce, in the normal way, using your *conscious* mind, it understands that you are simply 'practising' for when that moment arrives and in some mysterious way your subconscious then goes to work to help you make it happen. You may suddenly become more aware of things you had previously not paid much attention to and so on. And I suppose that's what we call intuition.

The first time I tried self-hypnosis I was feeling low in confidence and fearful of the future. I chose the affirmation 'I face all my problems with courage and enthusiasm and this helps me to solve them more easily.' But I decided that even this, relatively simple sentence, might be confusing for this particular exercise and changed it to, 'I face all my problems with courage. I am *filled* with courage.'

It was a good decision. The subconscious seems to respond better to very direct suggestions and within a couple of weeks I could feel my confidence growing. I could then choose one of the other affirmations. I now use this technique mostly for relaxation and 'healing' purposes. (I practise a form of healing called Reiki, which I may mention again later in the book.)

But here's what you should do. Please don't be put-off if it looks a bit complicated at first. It will soon become easy:

- Have your chosen item in mind and worded very simply
- Sit on a straight-back chair in a quiet room
- Keep both feet on the floor
- Let hands rest gently on your lap – palms up or down – whichever feels best
- Close your eyes
- Breathe deeply and gently
- When you breathe feel your stomach rise – not your chest
- Relax your whole body but don't slump
- I personally prefer to keep head erect but see how you feel
- Let any areas of tension reveal themselves and then 'allow' that tension to drift away – you might be able to visualise it moving out of your toes or fingertips like a coloured mist if that helps – but don't worry if you can't do that. Just let the tension drift away in any way it likes
- It should only take a minute or so to get to this point of relaxation
- Don't pay attention to any fleeting thoughts – just let them go
- Now start counting in your head – downwards from ten to one
- Visualise, if you can, going down a flight of steps as you count – again don't force this – just keep counting anyway
- Going deeper into a state of relaxation as the count goes on
- You may even 'hear' yourself saying things like, 'Going deeper – more relaxed' between some of the numbers
- Stop at ten and start repeating (in your mind) the affirmation you've chosen
- After just a short while – when you feel ready to do so – start counting again – upwards this time – from ten back to one
- This time you should try to feel yourself ascending and becoming more 'awake' and lively

- You can add to this feeling by saying – in your mind – things like 'feeling lighter and brighter' – between numbers
- Finish with something like, 'One – fully awake and full of energy'
- Then open your eyes and look around you with a feeling of well-being
- Then get up – perhaps take a sip of water and maybe some very gentle exercise – like a walk in the fresh air

And that's it. The whole thing can be done in less than ten minutes or you can go on for half an hour if that's what you want. And again it can be done as often or as rarely as you desire. I used to try and do it once a day but never any more than that.

I do it much less often that that these days. In fact I can sometimes achieve similar effects just be repeating the phrases again and again in my mind whilst I'm fully conscious – walking down the street, sitting in my dentist's waiting-room, or as I'm waiting to be introduced as a speaker. One of my favourite phrases to use in that last situation is: 'My heart is open. I am full of love for the people in this audience.'

And as crazy as that might seem it usually seems to have a positive effect. After a recent talk I gave to a writers' group a lady who'd been in the audience came to me and asked if I happened to be a Reiki practitioner. When I told her that I was she smiled happily and said, 'I thought so. I could see it in your aura. You were sending healing energy out to all of us.'

So was she just guessing – or was there something more to it than that? And what harm would it do anyway? Why not give it a try? Even if you're just about to address a small group at an interview or just an audience of one in a situation where you want to give a good impression of yourself?

But to get back to self-hypnosis for a moment – just as with the ordinary reading of affirmations – a single session a week is better than nothing at all. Once you've made progress in one personal development area then move on to another or just stop doing it for a while. Nobody's keeping score.

And just in case you're worried about any possible ill-effects self-hypnosis might cause I have to say I've never come across any myself. I find it a deeply relaxing and ultimately invigorating exercise that has long-term benefits for both mental and physical well-being.

Are there any dangers to self-hypnosis?

Don't worry. You won't be putting yourself into a deep trance and losing control. You'll be calm and relaxed but perfectly aware of whatever else might be going on around you. In fact you are likely to be *more* aware than you usually are because your mind isn't racing with countless thoughts and distractions.

But there is one possible danger that I must mention. There is a chance you'll relax so much that you might fall asleep.

So commonsense should tell you to bear this possibility in mind. Obviously you must choose a time and place that's appropriate. And I hope it goes without saying you wouldn't try this exercise when you have a meal cooking or children in your care or an appointment to keep. Only do it when you know it's perfectly safe to do so and preferably when there's another responsible adult on hand who knows what's going-on and will take-over if necessary.

But it can be a powerful tool. So keep that mind open and give it a try.

Points to note

Step Six

Use self-hypnosis

❖ Never underestimate the power of your subconscious mind
❖ Make sure *you* control your subconscious – not someone else
❖ Learn how to use this simple form of self-hypnosis to great effect
❖ Only use hypnosis to improve your own feelings and behaviour – not to attract 'things'
❖ Focus on developing one aspect of your personality at a time with this exercise
❖ Keep suggestions to your subconscious clear and simple
❖ Never focus on negatives when using self-hypnosis. Don't say 'I would like to lose my fear of interviews' but say instead, 'I am calm and full of confidence when being interviewed'

❖ This exercise promotes both mental and physical well-being
❖ Only use this exercise in an appropriate place and at an appropriate time
❖ Remember you may relax so much that you'll fall asleep. So don't take *any* risks
❖ Repeating positive affirmations in a fully-conscious state can also work wonders
❖ And once again it's supposed to be fun!

8 Make a Fresh Start

Dumping your unwanted baggage

AT THE BEGINNING OF A PREVIOUS chapter I used an analogy about travel agents so I'll continue along that track. Imagine that you've gone on the holiday of your dreams. A world cruise on the finest liner afloat. Naturally you've taken quite a bit of luggage. Now the sensible thing to do, once you're on the ship, would be to unpack all your cases and bags and put all your stuff in the appropriate places. Hang your suits or dresses in the wardrobe, place your shirts and blouses in drawers, and put your toothbrush in the bathroom. That's what sane people would do

But suppose, instead, you decided not to do any of that but carry your packed suitcases around with you for the entire voyage? You could stagger up and down the gangplank at every port of call, go into the dining-room for meals, dance around the ballroom or even try scuba-diving without ever letting go of two hundred and fifty pounds of luggage. (Or whatever you're allowed on a liner – I've only been on a ferry, a rowing boat and a troop ship) Does what I've suggested sound crazy? Nobody would dream of doing that. Right?

No they probably wouldn't because other people might notice and offer advice. (Or at least give them funny looks.) But in a sense that's exactly what many of us do with regard to our *mental* luggage. We take it with us everywhere.

Up to the clouds in an aeroplane or down to the bottom of the ocean in a submarine. We never let go of it and that can be just as much of a handicap to our emotions as 'real' luggage is to our bodies. Except of course that nobody really sees it. (Or at least that's what we kid ourselves into believing. And incidentally this invisible baggage can very quickly become harmful to the body too.)

But the one 'good' thing about real luggage is that it's almost bound to consist of things you are actually going to use at some time, whereas your mental luggage is all rubbish that's never going to do you any good.

And just in case you're still not convinced let me try another analogy. Imagine going to the cinema and watching a film you find disgusting, hateful and boring? Would you walk out before the film was over or stay to the very end? Most likely you'd stay to the end just to get your money's worth. (A paradox in itself – but generally true. Human beings are wonderfully strange creatures!)

But maybe that's fair enough. You might be hoping the film will have a brilliant ending. What you are *not* likely to do is to come back and pay to see that film again, the next night, and the one after that. And then buy it on dvd so you can play little bits of it over and over for the rest of your life.

Yet that's exactly what many of us do with our sad or disturbing memories. We replay them incessantly in our mind's-eye. We see them and hear them and get nothing positive from doing that at all. So why do it? That's like carrying around your entire luggage but filled with stuff you don't even like, that's worn out, doesn't fit you anymore and that you're *never* going to wear again. How crazy is *that*? So if we wouldn't do it in reality why do it at all? Why not simply trash the rubbish from our memories?

'Aah,' but I hear you say, 'It's not that easy.' Which brings us to an interesting point:

Who's in charge here?

If you find it difficult to stop thinking of something that upsets you, has that ever made you wonder who's controlling your thoughts? Is there a completely *separate* you that's outside your thoughts and looking-on like a spectator as your thoughts do just as they like? Does that make sense?

Perhaps it does? Perhaps there's a central part of your brain that loses control over other parts of the brain in the same way that it gradually loses control over parts of the body. As a soccer player I used to often drift past defenders as if they weren't really there. These days I'm more inclined to trip over defenders who *aren't* really there. So losing some measure of control over some of your thoughts seems to make sense to me.

And supposing it is true and perhaps you *can't* always be in complete control over every part of your brain and the thoughts it conjures up? Does that mean you have to passively accept that? No of course you don't. Just as I still do exercises to keep my body in reasonable shape I also do the same to help my thought processes.

This is quite a big subject and one, which I'll come back to in a later chapter so for now I'll focus on the matter at hand. How can you stop wasting your time and energy on mental garbage? I'll explain a couple of techniques that have worked like magic for me.

The scratched record technique

In case you are very young and don't know what a record is (or was) I should explain it was a bigger version of a cd but where the sounds were picked-up by a vibrating needle rather than a laser-beam (or whatever it is nowadays.) These discs could last for decades and I'm still playing some I first bought over fifty years ago but in fact, they are very vulnerable to rough handling.

In particular they can get scratched if you happen to jolt the record-player or knock the arm holding the needle so that it jumps out of the groove it's supposed to be following and slides across the disc. If the scratch is deep enough then every time you play that record in future it will flick the needle out of place and a different song will start play-ing. If there are several scratches the record becomes unplayable and as far as I know there's nothing you can do about it. You just throw the record away.

In a sense your repeated thoughts seem to wear an invisible groove in your brain – like the manufactured groove on a record that allows it to be played. Now just as we talked about you not wanting to keep a video of a film you hated why would you want to hang-on to the unpleasant happenings in your collection of memories? Why not get rid of them completely or at least render them unplayable?

I admit it isn't as simple to 'scratch' across a mental record as it is to do it to a physical object but it *is* possible. I know that because I've used these techniques – or my own version of them many times over the years.

Interestingly I very rarely have to use them now. If I find myself thinking negative thoughts these days I can just stop doing it at will. I simply remind myself I'm wasting my time and not enjoying myself.

It's a bit like being offered a drink at a party and having to choose between your favourite wine and a glass of dirty dishwater. Why would you choose the dishwater? And keep on doing it? (And why go to such a party in the first place!)

But many years ago when I *did* struggle to stop replaying bad memories in my mind I took action in the following manner. First of all I had to recognise that I was getting into a 'bad' record groove and become aware of it – rather than letting it sneak-up on me. Then I had to take some appropriate action immediately.

For example I've always found that negative thoughts seem to arise much more frequently when I'm sitting still rather than moving about. You can't simply avoid sitting down but you can force yourself to do something distracting the moment you need to. You can flick your mind on to another track just as the scratch on the record does it to the needle.

And since we're using that analogy I might as well mention one of the simplest things I do to change my train of thought. I actually start singing a song. A bright and breezy song or just one with happy associations for me. And sometimes I'll do a little tap dance as well. (Not a proper tap dance. Just my own made-up version. And I mean when I'm alone at home – not in a public library or travelling on a bus. Although that might work even better!)

But try feeling miserable when you're singing, 'Heaven, I'm in Heaven, and my heart beats so that I can hardly speak,' as you tap your way around the vegetable rack in the kitchen. Of course you won't *feel* like doing that if you are really low and it probably wouldn't be appropriate on every occasion (like in church during a funeral service for instance) but where it isn't going to offend someone else or make you feel shallow or disrespectful then give it a try. I promise you it works.

You simply can't feel two differing emotions at the same time. And even though you are only 'pretending' to be happy the part of your mind that wants you to be miserable doesn't realise you are only pretending. It can't get your attention. And the more times you use this technique the more automatic it will become. You will have 'scratched' the bad memory track and if you keep on doing it the whole sequence will eventually be destroyed.

Keeping busy

Keeping busy is an obvious 'avoidance' technique that many people adopt naturally. They throw themselves into their work or set about cleaning the house and so on. I love to go for a long walk. I find that walking stimulates my brain as well as my body. I also love to be out in open spaces away from buildings and crowds of people at times when I want some peace.

But if that's not for you make your own choices. It's important that you choose to do something you enjoy. You might not enjoy walking, singing or tap-dancing and prefer to tackle a crossword puzzle, look at your stamp collection, watch a dvd or listen to a favourite piece of music and that's fine if it works for you. But I've found that passive activities like this don't work for me. I have to get my body moving and start using some physical as well as emotional energy.

It probably goes without saying that it isn't a good thing to try 'drowning' your sorrows in alcohol or so-called recreational drugs. They'll only make you feel worse. The same goes for cigarettes. Get busy – get healthy. It's pure commonsense.

And something that can be even better than keeping busy just for your own benefit is helping someone else who really needs help.

Walking through Derby recently I bumped into a teacher friend of mine who had a big grin on her face. She'd just phoned her mother with an invitation to join her for lunch and been told it was impossible.

Her mother had promised to go and visit some 'old' people who were housebound and needed cheering-up. My friend's mother was eighty-four years of age at the time and she was going to help some 'old' people. What a great attitude! Can you imagine a woman like that sitting around feeling miserable? And I promise you her positive feelings show on her face and in her posture.

Does this all sound corny? So what? It works. Try it and see.

Acting 'as if'

Another well-known positive thinking technique that can work for me is to 'pretend' I'm happy and optimistic when I'm feeling miserable or 'pretend' I'm feeling fit and strong when I'm feeling a bit off-colour. And I do this when I'm with other people – not just on my own dancing in the kitchen.

If someone asks me how I am when I'm feeling low I don't tell them the truth I say something cheerful instead. 'I'm feeling great thanks,' or whatever. Now I know this seems to go against what I've included in my daily affirmations where one suggested item was about always being honest but it doesn't go against the *spirit* of what I'm trying to say.

When we talk about being honest we really mean we aren't going to tell lies that will mislead anyone in a harmful way. Nobody tells the absolute truth all the time. If we did it would cause chaos and we'd upset almost everyone we came into contact with.

In any case people '*know*' I'm exaggerating when I tell them how wonderful I'm feeling and how well life is treating me. But people have come to expect it from me and would be disappointed if I suddenly started telling them about the pain in my lower back or the fact that our television aerial needs replacing. In fact sometimes people smile at me before they even ask the question.

They probably think I'm a bit eccentric but by and large they seem to like it. And here's the best thing about it I actually feel better the minute I've said something positive. And unless I'm mistaken, so do they!

I read somewhere recently that medical research seems to prove that the one factor above all others that consistently effects a patient's chances of recovery is reflected in that person's attitude. I firmly believe this. At one point in her life my mother was only expected to live for a few weeks. She had a form of cancer. The doctor's involved at that time didn't realise what kind of person they were dealing with. My mother wasn't ready to die. She had too many things to do. She made a full recovery and lived for another twenty years. Always doing things for other people until she was practically worn-out.

You've probably all seen one of those party tricks where a person is asked to try and do something requiring physical strength after repeating a phrase like, 'I feel really weak and tired,' ten times. Then they struggle to do the task. But after repeating a phrase like, 'I feel full of energy and I'm very strong' ten times, they can do the task easily. Our bodies respond to how we feel emotionally and the things we say and the way we say them can change our feelings.

If we get into the habit of saying negative things a lot of the time then we'll feel weak and helpless a lot of the time. Obviously the opposite is true. We say lots of positive things and we feel better.

And I'm not just talking about saying positive things about yourself. It works in a similar way when you say positive things about other people. We all know people who do nothing but moan and groan all the time. Do these people seem happy to you? Are they as happy as the people who always have something nice to tell you or something complimentary to say about others?

And once again it's simply a matter of choice. As I've said before it's all to do with having the right attitude. Do you want to be miserable yourself and spread bad news around? Or would you rather choose happiness?

The power of forgiveness

Let me make something clear straightaway. I hesitated to use the word forgiveness here because as you'll see if you read on I'm not talking about forgiveness in the fullest sense of the word. I'm not saying you can ever shake someone's hand and say you wholeheartedly forgive him or her for some horrendous thing they may have done to you. In some cases that would be impossible.

But what I *am* saying is in those cases where it *is* possible and not entirely inappropriate then it's a wise and sensible thing to do. I'm sure you are capable of making your own decision about this. Various things might come into the equation: the seriousness of the incident, the degree of intent, any evidence of remorse and so on.

Taking all these things into consideration you may feel able to actually 'forgive' the person for whatever they did. That's the 'best' scenario.

You will not only be doing the other person a favour, you will be doing yourself a favour too. Bitterness eats away at you like a cancer. Get rid of it as quickly as you can.

There's an old Jewish saying that goes something like this: 'If someone hurts you once, then shame on them. If they hurt you again, shame on *you*.' This may be nothing more than a warning about not trusting people too much but I see it in another way.

Suppose someone hurts you and you spend the rest of your life being miserable about it and perhaps even plotting revenge? Then they've not only hurt you once or twice but possibly a thousand times.

And by hanging-on to the hurt and bitterness they caused you, you are working for them against yourself. It doesn't matter how serious the original offence against you was, the principle still holds good. In fact, the more serious the offence, the more benefit you'll derive from letting it go.

If you don't do that you are actively helping your persecutor to hurt you now and keep on doing it. They might even get pleasure from that if they know about it. How crazy is that?

But here's something that might be even crazier – they may not have known anything about your feelings against them in the first place. So whilst you were seething with anger at them for showing no remorse or perhaps because you thought they were gloating at their 'triumph' over you – they may have completely forgotten about the incident because it wasn't important to them.

I've talked about the best-case scenario but what about the worst? There can surely be nothing to compare with having something dreadful happen to one of your own children. Yet even here people's attitudes differ enormously.

A parent who's lost a child may feel he or she will never be able to smile again and will live the remainder of their life consumed by anger and bitterness as well as deep sorrow. And who can blame them?

Yet others will be galvanised into doing something positive – like setting-up a charity in their child's memory. It isn't difficult to see which attitude is going to work best for all concerned. The parents who simply can't ever forget their grief will not only be unhappy themselves but also will adversely affect the lives of everyone around them.

I'm not trying to cast blame here or say that I could go for the positive option whatever the circumstances. I wouldn't be so insensitive or presumptuous. But if some brave people can be positive in the most terrible of circumstances then surely most of us could do our best in more average ones?

So if you *can* forgive and it's appropriate then do it. As I've already said, you'll be doing *yourself* a favour as much as, if not more than, anyone else. If you can't forgive, or it's not appropriate, then isn't it better to *forget* or at least stop dwelling on it, and move on?

And please note: everything I've said about forgiving others applies equally to forgiving yourself. Don't waste time beating yourself up for the bad things you've done to others. What good will that do? You'll just make yourself unhappy and that, in turn, will affect others. Apologise to anyone you think would appreciate it or just put your mistakes out of your mind and resolve not to make so many in the future.

Be a better person and even if the good you do for others will never directly pay-off your debt to the person you really owe it to – it will still have a positive effect. An effect that can build-up and snowball and touch the lives of countless numbers of people in the years to come? This isn't fantasy. It's reality.

We all know of unhappy couples who've brought-up unhappy children, who've given them unhappy grandchildren, who've grown-up to marry other people from similar dysfunctional families and so on. But the opposite can also be true – and you can be a tiny part of *that*. If you have to forgive others and forgive yourself to achieve something wonderful isn't that a price worth paying? Think about it.

The high cost of never forgiving or forgetting

No need to give lots of examples here. Just think of the conflicts between Protestants and Catholics that have been going on for centuries and will never stop until enough people on both sides decide to call a halt. Until they decide to break the vicious circle and stop seeking revenge or wanting to have the last word.

As it happens my mother was an Irish Catholic and my father was an English Protestant. I never realised, until I was grown-up, how brave they must have been to marry and start a family together over eighty years ago at a time when 'the troubles' between Great Britain and Ireland were at a high point.

It wasn't easy for them. My mother came to England with my father and lost touch with her family for over twenty years. By the time she was reconciled, with her brothers and sisters, her father and stepmother had both died. What a high price to pay for falling in love with someone who other people regarded as an enemy.

And when I finally met my Irish Aunts, Uncles and cousins, many of them turned out to be warm and friendly, good-humoured and generous – in fact, pretty much like my English ones but with a different accent.

It might equally have involved people of a different race, culture or colour. We are all human beings and connected at a spiritual level that should transcend everything else. If you really want a happier future – get rid of your unhappy past. Make a fresh start and do it right now.

Points to note

Step Seven

Make a fresh start

- ❖ Mental baggage can be as heavy as ordinary baggage – carry it around and it wears you down
- ❖ Why hang-on to stuff you're never going to use anyway?
- ❖ If you saw a film on tv and hated it would you rush out to buy the DVD so you could watch it again.. and again?
- ❖ Decide who's in charge of your own thoughts
- ❖ Don't let your thoughts dig themselves deeper into a 'bad' groove
- ❖ Keep busy – by helping others you also help yourself
- ❖ Act 'As If' and spread happiness not misery
- ❖ Do yourself a favour – forgive others
- ❖ If you really can't forgive than try to forget – and move-on
- ❖ If someone hurts you once – then shame on them. If you hurt yourself a thousand times by thinking about it – then shame on *you*. Let it go. Whose side are you on?
- ❖ Remember the high cost of never forgiving or forgetting

9 Learn to Persist

One quality you can't do without

WHEN I WAS TEACHING SCRIPTWRITING AT Derby University I would sometimes ask a group of students on their very first session to write down five attributes they thought were necessary for anyone wanting to be a successful tv scriptwriter.

I wouldn't give them any clues or any time for discussion. I'd ask them to do this little task straight away. After a few moments I'd ask them to choose what they thought was the most vital item in their list and then raise their hand if they were willing to share it with the rest of us.

In the six years I taught this subject I don't remember anyone giving the answer I was hoping for – persistence – as their number one choice. More often than not it wasn't even included in their list at all. I'm not blaming the students for this. I had more or less 'tricked' them into this position. I'd allowed them to assume the answers I wanted were specifically relevant to the subject they were going to study.

So naturally they'd focus on things they knew we'd be practising during the course; like the ability to create memorable characters, to think in a visual way, to structure a story to fit within a certain time-slot and so on.

And this was all good stuff that we could usefully discuss later.

I hadn't 'tricked' them to make them look silly or to make myself look superior but simply to make the point more forcefully. To do it in a way they'd remember. I consider it *that* important because in my opinion without persistence the most talented writer is almost bound to fail.

Accounts of famous writers whose first efforts were rejected again and again are legendary. Type the words, 'Famous Author Rejections' on to your internet search engine if you don't believe me but let me give you the most striking example I could find – plus a more recent one.

Writers with persistence

British thriller writer John Creasey is reputed to have received the staggering figure of seven hundred and forty-three rejections before he made his first sale. And amazingly he then went on to sell five hundred and sixty-two books using more than a dozen different names. He became hugely successful for decades. Selling millions of copies of these books in various countries all around the world.

I must admit that when I first read about his rejections I thought it was probably a gross exaggeration. I also wondered about mentioning it in this book in case it put more people off than it inspired. But then I put my positive thinking head on and gave it a few moments quiet thought. I'd hazard a guess, for example, that all those rejections didn't involve novels – but mostly short stories. And I'm pretty sure also that they wouldn't all be *different* stories and that most, if not all of them, would have been submitted more than once.

So let's take it to extremes and guess that maybe each completely original story was rejected for anything up to five times?

That could bring the numbers down to a much more manageable one hundred and forty-eight and a third stories (let's be generous and call it one hundred and forty-nine shall we?) Which is only one story a week for less than three years. And if writing's your hobby that's not too daunting at all is it?

On the other hand he *did* have over five hundred complete *books* published so that's more than one book a month for more than forty years. Absolutely mind-boggling but if one person can have that much persistence can't the rest of us try just a few more times without getting discouraged?

Like, a much more recent author, JK Rowling for instance, whose first book in the Harry Potter series was rejected around twenty times before an acceptance that led to her becoming one of the richest women on the planet. After talking about hundreds of rejections twenty doesn't seem so bad at all does it? Surely any one of us could cope with that? But I'm afraid this isn't always the case because in my experience:

People give up too soon

I've personally given free and detailed advice to at least a dozen talented friends who've then given-up after their very first rejection. I'll repeat that. They've given-up after their *very first rejection*. In fact this is quite a common occurrence as far as I can tell.

I've taught hundreds of students in formal classes and at writers' events and only a very few of them have the ability to carry-on until they succeed. And what's true in this particular activity is true in general. The one vital ingredient for success is persistence. Raw talent is certainly not enough. I know dozens of people who are potentially better writers than I am and who have never sold a thing.

Some people complain that they are simply unlucky but you can't sit around waiting for your luck to change. Here's an expression I first heard at a seminar on scriptwriting run by American scriptwriting guru, Robert McKee. It's something else I used to tell my students, '*Never forget that one yes can wipe out a hundred no's.*' Do you think John Creasey would have agreed with that one?

And of course this doesn't just apply to would-be writers. By another of those coincidences that happen to me, as I was thinking about writing this particular chapter, I took a break to watch a tv documentary – it was about the life of a man who became a football legend.

The boy with 'no talent'

I'm sure even non-football fans will have heard of Bobby Moore who captained the England team to world cup glory in 1966. He was ranked as a great defender by some of the world's best players of the time. People like the Brazilian Pele and Portugal's Eusabio; yet ex-colleagues of his, appearing in the documentary, smiled in affection at his memory and said he had been blessed with little natural skill and was always a bit lacking in real pace. As a youngster he'd been chubby and one of the last boys to be picked for even a kickabout on the park.

Nobody (except perhaps his loving parents – his mother in particular) thought he had any chance of joining a professional team at any level – let alone becoming captain of the national side. And how did he do it? By sheer, controlled, application. Not by desperate efforts. He sought advice and than acted on it.

He practised and practised and studied so assiduously that he developed a sort of intuition about what other players would do. This kept him one step ahead, so his lack of speed was nullified.

On and off the pitch he always seemed composed and gentlemanly. And few people knew that he'd been battling – even *before* the World cup triumph – against the illness that would eventually take his life at a very young age. What an example of a natural positive thinker – of someone making the best of their life despite the most severe difficulties. Someone who really knew the value of persistence.

Famous people on persistence

Somebody once said to the late President Roosevelt's wife how lucky her husband had always been. She replied that yes that was true but added, 'And the strange thing is – the harder he works the luckier he gets.' It seems to me the president *was* lucky to have such a sensible wife. (Though I feel the need to remind you that this book isn't about working *harder* it's about doing more because you *enjoy* doing it. And I'm pretty sure that applied in the president's case too.)

This sentiment was echoed by another famous president who said, 'I am a slow walker, but I never walk backwards.' That was Abraham Lincoln. Yet another president, Calvin Coolidge said, 'Nothing in the world can take the place of persistence. Talent will not; nothing is more common than unsuccessful men with talent. Genius will not; un-rewarded genius is almost a proverb. Education will not; the world is full of educated derelicts. Persistence and determination alone are omnipotent.' And finally Albert Einstein said, 'It's not that I'm so smart. It's just that I stay with problems longer.'

Persistence not determination?

You may have noticed that, throughout this section of the book, I've used the word persistence rather then the more commonly used one, determination. I did it knowingly. I can't think of the word determination without also thinking of the phrase 'grim determination,' which isn't what this book is all about.

As I said right at the beginning I'm not trying to teach people how to win at all costs and be ruthless. I'm suggesting we can achieve things by enjoying what we do and without harming anyone else in the process. Indeed, by sharing our happiness with others.

Actually I've had a few students who've argued they can see no difference between these two words, persistence and determination, but you'll notice that President Calvin Coolidge used both words in the same sentence in the quote printed above. So obviously he agreed with me – that there is a difference.

I think of determination as being aggressive and persistence as being more passive and accepting. I imagine a persistent person gently asking for advice and then trying again but a determined person wanting to prove that they are right and you are wrong. (But then again I'd better practice what I preach here and say I may be wrong!) Just so long as you get the main point, which is to keep on keeping on, without making a nuisance of yourself or trampling over others.

My friend Chriss McCallum, author of the truly excellent *Writing how to articles and books* (published by Studymates), has just told me she doesn't even like the word persistence because it reminds her of the word 'pest'. She prefers to use 'perseverance' so there you are. (But she does agree with me on being wary of determination!)

Persistence: a personal example

I've given enough examples of things throughout this book , involving jobs, writing and football so I'll tell you an amusing little story about the one and only time I went skiing. (And yes Kranska Gora really is in Slovenia, which was part of the former Yugoslavia – not part of Switzerland! – so there's a bit of geography thrown-in for nothing.)

How the holiday came about was interesting in itself. One of the children had written a letter to a newspaper about my wife Pat being such a good mother and it won a prize when Pat was subsequently voted, 'Mother of the Year,' by a panel of judges from the newspaper concerned. The prize was a free holiday of her choice, for two people, anywhere in Europe. With the benefit of hindsight maybe it wasn't such a well thought-out prize because, how could such a good mother go off on holiday and leave all her children behind?

But that's where I decided positive thinking would come in useful and graciously volunteered to accept the holiday on her behalf. (But don't worry we all went to Florida some time later.) Anyway I took one of our sons, Simon, who was then fourteen and his nephew Shaun who was five years older, as an added extra. They had both shown some interest in the idea of skiing and that's the holiday that appealed to *me* most at the time.

We discovered a slight problem when we got there. There was no snow. That is, no 'real' snow but there was a machine creating something that looked a pretty good imitation to me. But there wasn't enough to go around. There was one huge slope covered in white surrounded by green and brown hills.

This white slope was usually reserved for complete beginners and novices but now it was being used by everybody. Olympic standard performers were doing somersaults (literally), and groups of school-children and downhill racers were all jostling for space on the one rather icy slope. And it was intimidating. Not only did it seem danger-ous but it was embarrassing; to be making a fool of yourself, in front of dozens, if not hundreds of other people.

Several people on our complete beginners' course lost interest on the very first day and went off to do other things. Simon and Shaun stuck it out for nearly a week of our ten-day holiday, but were hating it. I didn't blame them at all. They were both excellent athletes who were used to doing well on the sports field but here they were (as they imagined) being shown-up by old age pensioners and little toddlers who'd no doubt been skiing for years.

But it was the day I fell off the chair-lift halfway up the slope and slid all the way down knocking about six other people off who were on the chairs behind me, that really did it. When we all landed in a tangled heap back at the start of the queue. I looked up to see Simon and Shaun pretending that, not only were they not with me but they couldn't even speak English. That's when I just knew it wasn't really working.

They stayed away from the slope after that and went ice-skating and chatting-up girls in the cafes instead. Even the ice-skating was new to them but at least they didn't have to risk stabbing a schoolchild with one of their ski sticks as they completely lost control and slid into a crowd of people.

But I still wanted to ski from the very top of the slope to the bottom – just like I'd seen people do in the movies and just like I'd dreamed of doing since I was a youngster myself. Now I was actually there it was something I just *had* to do.

I had a feeling I would never get another chance because – like the two lads – I hadn't really enjoyed it that much. On the final day of the holiday I waited until the crowds had thinned out and then got on the chair-lift. I was practically the only passenger. I stayed on it as it reached the point where beginners usually got off, and went all the way to the summit. I wasn't sure if real beginners were even allowed to do that but there was nobody watching me. I dismounted and stood a bit shakily on a flat piece of land, looking down at people who looked like tiny ants in the far distance.

I couldn't help wondering if I'd do what one beginner had done a few days earlier. He'd picked-up so much speed that he'd gone right across the flat area at the bottom of the slope, off the snow, and on to a patch of icy grass before crashing through a wooden barrier into the gravelled carpark. He'd broken a bone in his arm and he'd achieved all that after starting from the learners' spot, not the top of the slope.

I began to wonder if I'd be forced to beat that and, go all the way through the car-park, across the main road and join the two lads for a coffee and a slice of cake in one of the cafes. I still hadn't quite got the hang of travelling at speed without brakes though I knew what you were supposed to do in theory.

I plotted a course in my mind, near one edge of the slope, that avoided people altogether, and hoped I'd hit a few patches of softer snow. So many people had been using the main part of the slope that the snow was almost like ice in some places.

I decided to stop worrying anymore and simply go for it. Halfway down I suddenly felt I'd finally 'got' it. I stopped thinking with my brain and let my body take over. It really was exhilarating and I only wish the two youngsters had been able to experience it. At the bottom I had enough space to swing around in a great arc before coming to a halt still on my feet.

I looked around, half-expecting a round of applause but of course nobody had even noticed. But I was glad I'd done it and once again I'd had confirmation that positive thinking (and persistence) really works.

And telling this little story reminds me of another very useful technique I learned on that course for scriptwriters run by Robert McKee. It takes us right back to 'attitude' once again:

The 'pebble on the beach' strategy

Maybe John Creasey used this technique automatically in order to endure all those rejections and it's certainly something I urged all my students to try. It's a way of disassociating yourself from anything you've written so that you don't feel personally under attack if someone is critical of it.

You realise that the critic is commenting on the writing as if it's an object completely separate from you. As if, for example, it's a pebble picked-up on a beach.

So suppose for a moment you actually have picked up a pebble from a beach and you think it's beautiful. It's an unusual colour and has a veined pattern like a piece of marble. It feels warm and smooth to the touch.

But when you show it to a companion he gives you a slightly puzzled look and says: 'It's just an ordinary pebble. Throw it away.'

Would you get angry with him and start arguing about it or would you burst into tears because you feel insulted? Would you then feel so stupid and disappointed that you'd throw the pebble away and never look at another pebble again? Unless you are super-sensitive it's very doubtful.

Most likely you would calmly agree to differ and quietly wish your companion had better taste. But you wouldn't want to deny him the right to have his own opinions. You might even look more closely at the pebble to see if there was any merit in what your companion had said. But I repeat: you wouldn't feel *insulted*. You would quietly persist in holding to your own opinions.

And that's precisely the attitude you need to have when submitting a piece of writing to a publisher or a producer or an editor. Or indeed, when attempting to do *anything* in life that you are going to be judged on. I don't want you to think this part of the book is aimed exclusively at writers. The principles involved hold good for you, whatever you want to be: a business tycoon, a bricklayer, a butcher, a baker or a candle-stick maker.

You have made something or attempted something that you are proud of. *You* like it or you wouldn't have shown it to anyone else or told anyone else about it, and now you want to know what *they* think. You're willing to listen and learn. You are discussing an object, or an action you've taken – not your entire value as a human-being.

If you think this is a difficult thing to do you are absolutely right – at first. But if you think it's impossible then you are absolutely wrong. I know because I can do it quite easily after years of practice.

Even friends and relatives don't always believe me when I ask their opinion on something I've written (like the early drafts of this book for instance) and I stress that I want the truth as they see it.

I explain to them that well-meaning but misguided flattery won't teach me anything and may hinder my progress by sending me in the 'wrong' direction. But still they are sometimes reticent – afraid to offend me. They will say things like, 'What do I know? I'm not a writer.' But I'm not asking them to *write* something I'm asking them to read something – and they *are* readers. Just like all the millions of other people out there that I'm aiming at.

So people who refuse to give an honest opinion on something you've asked them about aren't being kind or helpful. They are projecting their own fears of criticism on to you. And unfortunately these fears are very prevalent.

Welcome advice and criticism

I've lost count of the number of would-be writers I've unwittingly offended over the years. And this, despite, the lengths I'll go to in trying to be both sensitive and constructive. People just *are* too easily put-off. I promise you this is true. I could give dozens of examples but I'll give just one that I'm sure will make the point well enough.

A close friend of one of my sisters had made an attempt at writing a tv script. She asked my sister if she thought I might give an opinion on it. My sister said that I probably would, because I am willing to give an opinion on almost anything, even without being asked. She also said that I'm a bit of a soft touch who finds it hard to say no. But she then warned her friend not to go through with it.

My sister has a cutting sense of humour and said to her friend, that, in her opinion, I am secretly being paid by other writers to cut down the competition, by putting people off writing for ever. She said that every time I give an opinion on a script or book (done by a complete beginner – not a serious student) the person involved disappears and is never heard off again. But her friend just laughed and passed on her script anyway.

I called her on the phone and explained as gently as possible that I could either read the script and give her some general advice and encouragement or I could treat her like a student and give detailed comments. I said that in either case I wouldn't lie to her. I would tell her the truth.

She was delighted with this and assured me that she wanted the real deal with no holds barred. She had already contacted a script-doctoring service and been told it would cost her quite a sum of money to have her manuscript looked at. I had said I'd do it for nothing because she was a friend of the family. She insisted there was absolutely no way she'd be anything but grateful.

I spent the whole weekend and then several evenings poring over the script and was reasonably impressed. The basic idea was very promising and the two main characters were engaging. But the structure was weak and the main storyline sometimes got lost. There were far too many characters and occasional a confusion about who was the focal character anyway. But it had definite signs of promise.

I wrote comments (in pencil so they could easily be erased) on page after page and then a glowing overall report at the end. Then I drove to her house with the manuscript, gave it to her, went home, and waited for her response. That was several years ago and I'm still waiting.

As far as I know that lady *still* isn't speaking to my sister anymore. (And it might be nice to think I'll be getting a cheque through the post from some mysterious mafia-style group of writers who don't want any more newcomers on their turf – but I won't be. I really tried to help.) But as I say – people just don't take criticism very well and it's so sad.

Do people *really* laugh at hopeful beginners?

As I've already implied, what's true with regard to a piece of writing can be equally true in other situations. Like learning to ski for instance. You can still use the pebble on the beach strategy here. If people are critical of your ability as a skier they're not dismissing you as a person. Would you dismiss your own child, or indeed, anyone else's, because he or she wasn't born with the ability to walk and talk?

Unless you're a natural bully of course you wouldn't. On the contrary you would find them endearing and lovable and want to help and encourage them. Isn't that quite likely the attitude people will take towards you, whatever your age, as you try to learn something new?

My son Simon and my nephew Shaun were so embarrassed by doing something badly, as beginners, performing in front of experts, that they simply stopped doing it. I don't blame them for this at all. As a teenager myself I was much worse.

I still remember refusing to go to my father's works Christmas party unless he promised I wouldn't have to collect my present from Santa Claus in public. I couldn't even bear the thought of people hearing my name being called out and then watching me climb up two steps before walking a few paces across a tiny stage on my own.

So I know how my son and my nephew felt on the ski slope. But I wish I could have changed their minds. In reality none of the expert skiers gave a damn about watching a bunch of learners. Why should they? They too had once been learners.

And as for the other beginners – well they were too busy worrying about themselves. In fact it got to a point where I was deliberately drawing attention to my own inadequacies to spare other people's blushes. It made me quite popular and did me no harm at all. I was the 'crazy' Englishman who got invited to sit at other people's tables and share their bottles of wine. And I still managed to ski further than almost all the others in that beginners' group.

I'm not trying to be boastful here. I'm just telling you how it was. I could have felt shy and uptight as I would have done once upon a time but I chose to relax, enjoy myself and *persist*. I eventually achieved more than I would have done otherwise and I also helped to create a 'good' atmosphere in the process.

Doesn't that make perfectly good sense to you? So don't worry about what other people *might* be thinking. (Because you're probably wrong anyway!) Just focus on what you want to achieve.

Points to note

Step Eight

Learn to persist

* Persistence is the one quality you can't do without
* Many people give up too soon
* One Yes can cancel out a hundred No's
* Remember how a boy with 'no' talent became a legend
* You can be a slow walker – but don't walk backwards
* 'Nothing in the world can take the place of persistence' Calvin Coolidge
* If you're shy try the 'Pebble on the beach' strategy
* Flattery is very nice but it can send you in the wrong direction
* Welcome criticism and advice – you can learn from them both
* Don't assume that people will look down on you as a beginner
* Would anyone sneer at a toddler who was learning to walk?

10 Learn by Experience

Don't get bogged down with theory

AS I'VE SAID BEFORE I'M NOT much of an intellectual. I like things to be explained to me in a simple and straightforward way. I remember sitting in a lecture room one day when I was training to be a teacher and being told to make a note of the following quote: 'A child learns, through a process of assimilation and accommodation, to maintain his (or her) dynamic equilibrium.'

This was a quote, based on a theory proposed by a famous Swiss psychologist called Piaget. I dutifully wrote it down, as did all the other students. (We were all *mature* students and a pretty well-behaved group for most of the time.)

But the lecturer must have noticed my slightly pained expression and asked me what was wrong. I politely asked him what the quote actually meant. He was a good teacher and a decent enough man but on this occasion his response was ever so slightly sarcastic. He asked me if I knew what the words 'assimilation', 'accommodation', and 'dynamic equilibrium' meant.

I said that I thought I had a pretty good idea. 'So what do you *think* the quote means?' he asked. 'I *think*' I said, adding a tinge of sarcasm to my own tone, 'It means, a child learns by experience.' 'So what are you complaining about?' he asked. 'I'm not complaining,' I said, 'Just wondering why he didn't say it like that.'

And in case you think I was just being obnoxious here's a quote I remember from the late Malcolm Muggeridge (who certainly *was* an intellectual compared with me). As far as I can recall he was writing in a newspaper, about sociology, when he gave a definition something like this: 'Sociology is the study of groups of people who don't need to be studied – by people who do.'

The point I'm trying to make is that although academic study is vital there is only so much a person can learn by theory alone. (Especially, in my opinion, when those theories are couched in an unnecessarily pompous kind of way.)

Some things simply have to be learned by *doing* them. Try learning to drive a car, ride a bicycle, play the piano, or swim across the channel by reading books about them or attending lectures and taking notes.

And even if you become a real expert on something then the only way to extend the boundaries on what you know or what you can do, is by taking chances. And however well-informed and sensible you are it's still almost certain that you'll make mistakes.

Just remember that theory is fine – but it's practice that makes perfect. Here's an important lesson I learned about the *value* of making mistakes. It's an example I gave in my book, *Writing TV Scripts* but it actually happened when I was writing a stage play.

Making mistakes

This is a slightly altered version of what I wrote in the book I've just referred to: "One of the wisest things anyone ever said to me about learning to write came from the then Artistic director at the Derby Playhouse Studio, David Milne.

We'd been working together on a comedy play called 'Adult Pantomime' and having lots of problems. I'd write a sequence, get it photo-copied and we'd present it to the six actors. They'd try to act it out, make suggestions, and then throw the discarded pages in the wastebasket. Then I'd go away to do the re-writes and we'd go through the same process again, until at one point, David discarded the wastebasket, and replaced it with a plastic dustbin.

He saw my look of dismay and asked if he'd put me off. I said not exactly but I'd know it was time to quit when he replaced the dustbin with a skip. The re-writes and the suggestions carried on until eventually we had a script that was workable. (And turned out to be quite successful.)

But the really funny thing was that having started off with a fairly complex idea we finally settled on a pretty straightforward script about half the length of the original. I looked at the final script and said to David, 'Why didn't I just write it like this in the first place?' And he said to me, 'For the same reason that the person who invented the Penny Farthing Bicycle didn't invent a multi-speed mountain bike. It just doesn't work like that.'

It was brilliant advice and I've remembered it ever since. You simply can't go from nothing to something special without wading through a lot of junk. So expect to clear the rubbish from your mind before you can produce something good. *That's* the way it works."

David was absolutely right. And what applies to writing, no doubt, applies to almost everything else you might try for the first time. I'm sure you've all heard the expression, 'You can't make an omelette without breaking a few eggs.'

(And actually I can't make a really good omelette even *after* breaking a lot of eggs – but I'm sure I could learn if I practised even more.)

Some famous 'mistakes'

So it's pretty clear there are two ways you can look at your mistakes. You can either see them as stumbling-blocks or stepping-stones. Again it's a question of attitude and again it's your choice.

You probably will recall how Christopher Columbus set off to find a new route from Europe to India but found America instead (and how's that for an example of what a 'mistake' can lead to?) but did you also know that a man called Strauss went to America to look for gold and didn't find any but still got rich anyway?

Because what he *did* find were lots of other prospectors who needed some tougher clothing than the stuff they'd brought with them or that they could buy from stores. This failed prospector saw his opportunity, started making trousers from a type of canvas and ended-up creating the massively successful Levi Strauss Jeans company.

Then there was the great inventor Thomas Eddison who tried more than *six thousand* different filaments in his attempts to create the world's first electric light bulb before someone suggested he might be wasting his time. He replied that he hadn't wasted his time experiencing six thousand failures, he had used his time well *discovering* six thousand ways that didn't work.

Amazingly, and quite correctly as it turned out, he was able to see that as a positive thing and press-on with his experiments. And he still had a very long way to go.

He actually went on to 'discover' almost four thousand *more* ways that didn't work – until he finally discovered one that did. And how useful has that discovery been to countless millions of people throughout the world?

And I realise that example could just as easily have been in the section on persistence so to twist the phrase I quoted from Robert McKee's seminar in the previous chapter, we could say: 'One success can wipe out a hundred failures,' or in Thomas Edison's case, almost *ten thousand* failures. Doesn't that make you feel humble? Doesn't it make the meagre efforts of all those people who give up on their ambitions after their very first attempt look a bit ludicrous?

But having said that please note that little word *can* in the sentence I quoted (or mis-quoted). There really are no guarantees on *anything* you do. Very few people would have the persistence of men like John Creasey and Thomas Edison and that's hardly surprising. What they did seems to verge on craziness.

They must have been very sure of themselves indeed to stay *that* focussed on their goals. There surely must come a time when it makes sense to quit? The trouble is – how do you know when that time has arrived?

Knowing when to quit

In my own case I start thinking I'm wasting my time – and therefore wasting my life – when I stop *enjoying* the challenge and find I'm *only* focussing on the possible result – a result that might never be achieved.

That's when I listen to my inner feelings and ask myself if I'm *really* doing something I'm *supposed* to be doing or if I'd be better employed doing something else. Then I have a difficult decision to make.

But if all that all seems a bit vague and woolly-minded for you then you might like to hear about a little method I came-up with to help me at such times of confusion. I promise you it works. (Well it works for me – and you should know what that means by now!)

Learn how to make a 'no-lose' decision

Perhaps I first ought to mention something I learned from Susan Jeffers excellent book, *Feel The Fear And Do It Anyway*. First published by Arrow Books in 1991. ISBN 0-09-974100-8.

I like Susan's idea for making what she calls, a 'No Lose' decision, because it's so simple. I'll make it even simpler here by just giving the basics. Susan explains that when we are torn between making a decision between, say, two differing courses of action we tend to see either choice as a win/lose one. We hope we've made the 'right' decision but can't help constantly worrying that we've actually made the 'wrong' one instead.

That hinders any progress we are likely to make as we spend time trying to work out what 'might' have happened if we'd made the other choice. But of course, with an attitude like that, it's highly probable that the very *same* thing would have happened. By thinking that either choice could be the 'wrong' one we are putting doubts and fears into our mind.

As Susan says it's a lot more sensible to see both choices as win/win ones and act 'as if' they are. Make-up your mind to concentrate on that choice and learn from it no matter what happens. Forget what *might* have happened if you'd made the other choice.

As I see it you're making a declaration of intent by acting in this way. You've made your choice so at that point it *is* the right one. You just have to make sure it stays that way and stop worrying about what might have been. Who can ever know what might have been anyway?

Which takes me right back to the tragic deaths of my friend Bryan and his family members. Sometimes people who know about what happened on that fateful day shake their heads in sadness but then say how lucky I was not to have been with Bryan at the time (as I was supposed to be.) But I point out to them that if I *had* been there then every single detail of that holiday would have been altered.

Think about it for a moment. Isn't it almost impossible to imagine that the presence of three more people, even if they were travelling in a separate car, would have made no difference to a complicated sequence of events that put the accident vehicles in that precise position on a particular road at a particular time?

So if I hadn't acted so badly towards my first wife then we'd have gone on the holiday with my friend and his family and they might all have still been alive to this day. Yes I've actually thought of it in those terms. But I can't beat myself up about it. As I say, who's to know *what* would have happened given a different set of circumstances?

You simply can't predict the future in such precise detail and you certainly can't change the past so it's futile to even think about it. A thousand little equations might have prevented that accident from happening the way it did. A few minutes extra spent at a petrol station – someone feeling hungry and wanting to stop for a sandwich – anything at all.

But let's get back to decision-making. As I say, Susan's idea is perfectly fine for making a decision between one of two choices. But I needed an idea that dealt with a more complex situation. Something to use when you have a variety of options to choose from. I'm really quite proud of this idea I came-up with. Not only does it work but it can actually be good fun using it.

As far as I can recall it just came to me out of the blue one day, when I was feeling over-stretched with ideas on writing and I couldn't make-up my mind what to actually focus on for a certain period. My wife, Pat and some of the older children were fed-up with me mooching about – keeping so busy doing nothing – that I had no time to do anything else. So here's what that led to:

Making difficult decisions

First of all I started by making a list of the options I'd been considering. Here it is:

- Write a tv sitcom pilot episode
- Write a tv comedy/drama pilot episode
- Write a radio sitcom pilot
- Write a one-off radio drama
- Write more short stories
- Write another stage play
- Write a novel

I then made a second list of the criteria I would use to help me make my judgement:

- How good am I at doing this?
- How much do I really want to do it?
- What are the opportunities like?
- What is the payment like?
- Will my wife and family be supportive on this?

I then transferred these two columns to a simple grid I drew on a sheet of paper, like the much neater one you can see at the back of this book. There was no need to write the sentences out in full to know what each column was for.

Then as you will see I gave each option a score out of ten. Ten being the most positive score each time and nought being the most negative. I added the scores and put the totals in the end column on the right-hand side. And obviously the scores show at a glance which appears to be the 'best' option. So far so good.

But it doesn't end there. One of the real blessings of this method is the way it can show immediately how some options are complete non-starters at that particular time. You'll see this clearly applies to four items on my chart. I immediately dropped these four. (Though I did, come back to each of them later – with some successes apart from novel writing so far.)

And having four fewer options to think about was really helpful in that situation. And as you'll see my 'top' choice at the time was for Radio Sitcom which I did then concentrate on and which did lead to my biggest break as a writer up till then.

This exercise convinced me that sometimes 'non-starter' options can niggle away at the back of your mind for ages, taking-up valuable thinking time.

Before I came-up with this method I would, sometimes, consider totally unsuitable options again and again without being able to come to a firm decision. But once I saw them set out in this stark manner it became perfectly obvious that I could banish them from my thoughts – at least for the time-being – without a qualm.

And of course there can sometimes be a very clear winner. If there isn't, as in the case illustrated, then I'll sometimes re-check the scores given to each item and maybe even add another category.

But it doesn't need to end there either. Whether there's a clear winner straight away or not there's still another step to take. (I told you it was fun!) There's a final twist that always amuses me.

Rather than just accept the 'winner' I will sit quietly for a moment and assess how I feel about it. If I'm happy and energised I just get on with it but if I feel a slight sense of disappointment and find myself wanting to check the scores again – or even alter some of them to get a different result – then I know I've subconsciously made my decision anyway. Then I won't rest until I've 'fiddled' the scores to get the result I *really* want and that's great. I can act on that final decision with enthusiasm.

The strange thing is I can't just reason this out without going through this little 'game'. It really does clarify things for me. And I enjoy doing it. Try it and see if it works for you. Obviously you'll need to come-up with your own list of choices and criteria to judge them by but that's a good exercise in creative thinking anyway and it all adds to the fun.

Please note that the scores I've given to each option are very personal ones – based on my own feelings at the time – not necessarily on hard facts. My chart as illustrated was very personal to me, and all to do with writing but I've used the idea for other things too.

Here's a few problems you might like to consider using it for: buying a house, changing your job, buying a new car, going on holiday, buying a holiday home, starting-up your own business, beginning or ending a relationship, or even starting a family.

These are all areas where your judgement can get clouded by the number of factors to consider – especially if you simply jump from one to another without seeing the complete picture set-out clearly in front of you. Just to make the process absolutely clear it goes like this:

1. Make a list of your options
2. Make a list of the questions you'll use to judge them on
3. Put these details on a grid – as illustrated
4. Give marks out of ten to each question posed (making sure you always mark high for the positive – rather than the negative implications) and total the points
5. Dump the 'non-starters' for the time being – to clear your mind
6. If there's no outright winner – review the points given on each category
7. (And check your arithmetic anyway – just in case!)
8. Add another category to judge by if necessary
9. Do this until you *can* decide on a winner
10. Sit and think about the winner for a while – just a few minutes

11. If you feel good about it – you have your answer
12. If you feel unsure – go through part of the scoring procedure again
13. If you are *still* unsure then consider the following observations:

Leaving your comfort zone

You may find yourself, as I sometimes do, at this point in the above exercise, wanting to 'cheat' in favour of a particular option that keeps failing to get the highest score – no matter how much you juggle the figures. If that's the case then you've probably made your decision at a subconscious level but are scared of recognising it for some reason.

You might, for example, be more afraid of success, than failure. It may surprise you to learn that many people are. They are subconsciously afraid to leave their perceived 'comfort-zone.'

You might be holding yourself back because you think you don't deserve whatever it is you really want. (If this applies to you then use your daily affirmations to widen your comfort zone by including something like: 'I now truly deserve all the good things that come to me.')

Maybe you have some deep desire that excites and scares you so much that you didn't even include it on your chart in the first place? And I'm sure you'll realise I'm only talking of 'positive' and worthwhile things here. I'm not encouraging you to cross the Sahara Desert on a pogo-stick or try to reach the North Pole wearing flip-flops and it should go without saying that I'm not talking about something illegal or unpleasant.

But I know from my experiences as a teacher, lecturer and foster-parent, how many people, both young and old, consistently undervalue their own potential. Why shouldn't you try to achieve something wonderful? What harm will it do to yourself and others if you try and don't succeed? Especially if you enjoy making the effort and know that other people aren't going to suffer in the process.

Anyway, once you have made your final decision take Susan Jeffers advice and see it as a win/win decision. Forget about any other decision you could have made – for the time being – and move forward. Learn from your mistakes. And remember this:

You can't avoid making decisions:

You are *always* making decisions. There's no such thing as *not* making a decision. If you decide *not* to make a decision then that's a decision in itself.

It might even be the 'right' one for a while but a very negative one if you do nothing for too long. So make important decisions with courage and be prepared to learn from your mistakes. *See your mistakes as stepping-stones – not stumbling-blocks.* And if you can do this *and* see your life as an adventure you'll not only enjoy it more but you may end-up finding something even better than the thing you *thought* you were looking for.

Points to note

Step Nine

Learn by experience

- ❖ Theory is fine – but it's practice that makes perfect
- ❖ You can't make an omelette without breaking a few eggs
- ❖ Never forget that one 'Yes' can wipe out a hundred 'No's'
- ❖ It *might* be time to quit when you stop enjoying the challenge
- ❖ Learn how to make a 'no-lose' decision
- ❖ Sometimes fear of success is a bigger problem than fear of failure
- ❖ Many people under-value their own potential
- ❖ Not making a decision might be the *right* decision – but not for too long
- ❖ Listen to your inner-feelings for guidance
- ❖ Keep your decisions positive
- ❖ See your mistakes as stepping-stones not stumbling-blocks
- ❖ Don't worry about what might have been – focus on what still might be

11

Make Use of Coincidence

Meaningless or meaningful?

CARL JUNG, THE FAMOUS SWISS PSYCHIATRIST, certainly believed that coincidences could be meaningful. He came-up with a new word, synchronicity, to describe them. He also believed, as I do, in an invisible force that connects us all. He called it the collective unconscious.

It's only fair to say that some cynics claim that Jung's ideas in this area are nonsense and that coincidences are just random happenings until people start to attribute 'false' meanings to them. They point out – quite rightly – that human-beings have a great skill at seeing connections where none exist. I don't argue with this.

You may remember, some years ago there was a sudden craze for what were called 'magic eye' pictures. What at first, seemed to be nothing more than splodges of colour or random patterns, would suddenly transform into three-dimensional, pictures that could be quite enchanting.

In a sense, of course, those pictures actually *were* there. They'd been put there by design but I can just as easily make pictures appear on the marbled tiles in my bathroom. I do it for my own amusement, as I lie soaking in the bath. It sometimes intrigues me that the pictures I conjure-up can vary according to my mood at the time.

I may see the outstretched wings of an angel, a clown riding on an elephant, or the leering face of a demon and all from the same pattern on differing occasions.

And sometimes even I'm surprised by this. Especially if I hadn't consciously realised that I was feeling, happy, jolly or a bit depressed, before creating the picture. So yes, the cynics may have a point. Maybe we do attribute meanings where there are none?

Perhaps, as they claim, there are so many opportunities for coincidences to happen that a certain number are bound to happen to every single person from time to time. And perhaps we do pay undue attention to the ones that seem to have some 'meaning' to us and ignore all the others. But to state categorically that *all* coincidences are meaningless, as some cynics do, is almost as unlikely an assertion as to say the opposite and claim that all coincidences are important and must mean something vital.

I like to keep an open mind on this. Lots of things that are happening right now will be moving towards things that are going to happen in the future. This is simply cause and effect. A team of workers stacking bricks and timbers on a piece of land, for example, will usually produce a house or some other kind of building. And we understand that. But suppose we *didn't* understand it.

Suppose you'd lived all your life as a wandering nomad, living off the land and sleeping in a tent, an igloo or some other kind of makeshift dwelling? Then perhaps you'd have no idea what to expect from a group of men digging holes in the ground and filling them with wet cement.

You might think to yourself, 'I wonder why those people are making such a mess of this place? It would be the perfect spot to set-up a camp for the winter.' And if you went back there later and found a row of houses with people living inside them and smoke coming out of the chimneys you might think it was just a happy coincidence. You'd thought of people living there in some kind of community and there it all was. And that might happen more than once over a long period of time before you made the logical connections.

Now you may think this is a silly example for me to give. So I'll give an even sillier one. Suppose you weren't a human-being at all but a frog or an earthworm? Would the situation make any sense to you at all? If a human picked you up and tried to explain it all to you, would you understand it? Would you accept that something with greater intelligence than yourself was controlling things?

I think it's doubtful. There would be things going-on around you that you simply couldn't begin to understand. And isn't it possible that we humans have similar limitations? Similar difficulties in understanding things beyond our experience and predicting what they might lead to?

Suppose the universe and everything that happens in it isn't just a series of random happenings at all but a kind of cosmic jigsaw-puzzle? Something that makes perfect sense to someone or *something* beyond our understanding?

And suppose we might occasionally learn more about these patterns ourselves just as the wandering nomads would quickly learn about builders and building sites. Maybe we are sometimes clever enough or lucky enough to get a better inkling of the possible consequences of the actions we take and the situations we set in motion – just as we might catch a glimpse of a picture on the box that contains a jig-saw puzzle?

So to come back down to Earth and put this in more practical terms we might notice a coincidence and then think to ourselves, I wonder what other piece in the cosmic jigsaw-puzzle I should be looking for to connect with these two pieces?

And if you find something, and then go on to find something else, what might eventually emerge when enough of those pieces are fitted together? Looked at in this light then perhaps so-called psychics aren't 'magic' at all and aren't simply making guesses but are people who can 'read' a set of complex and inter-connecting circumstances much better than the rest of us?

Maybe being psychic just means being more intelligent in a specific area of knowledge – simply being more sensitive? And that's something we can develop.

I told you right near the beginning of this book how a strange series of coincidences led me towards the writing of it. So taking coincidences seriously certainly seemed to work for me. It helped me achieve one of my lifetime dreams.

Maybe it can help to do the same for you if you'll only give it a try? In the hope of persuading you further I'm going to tell you of a few more coincidences I've been involved with over the years. And I'm also going to hazard a guess each time as to what these happenings *might* have been trying to tell me.

And I say once again this isn't complicated theory and conjecture. These are simple accounts of things that actually happened. Let the cynics claim that I'm fooling myself. Just make-up your own mind about it.

The street name

We had been living in an unfamiliar district for just a few days and I was walking around to get some exercise and to enjoy having a closer look at the surroundings. I particularly liked the look of one narrow street, about three-quarters of a mile from our new house.

It was half-hidden behind a busier street and along the boundary of some hospital gardens. At one end the street narrowed into a wooded footpath. It was almost like something you might see in a Walt Disney movie.

When I got to the end of this street I looked for a name-plate because I wanted to tell my wife Pat about this surprisingly pleasant row of houses when I got home. But to my surprise there wasn't a name-plate.

For some reason I was so disappointed by this that instead of carrying-on in the direction I'd intended I turned around and walked all the way back to the 'beginning' of the street to see if there was a nameplate there. There was. It said on it, 'Owlers' Lane'. I smiled at this because it struck me as a strange name that seemed somehow appropriate.

As far as I can remember I didn't consciously make a mental note of any other street names on my long and circular walk and I certainly didn't walk along any other street more than once, looking for a name-plate.

I arrived home to find my wife Pat in a bit of a flap. One of our young daughters had been invited to a birthday party and been given an address but no telephone number. Pat couldn't find the street on the map and our new neighbours had never heard of it. Our daughter sat there in her party frock looking glum. The party was almost about to start. And of course you know what's coming. We bundled her into the car and shot off towards 'Owlers' Lane.'

Was that meaningless or not? Certainly it wasn't of world-shattering importance. But it gave me a warm glow. I decided, there and then, it was a sign that we'd made the 'right' choice in moving to that district and that we'd be happy there. And we were. We were very happy. The neighbours were delightful and we only moved when another foster-child came along and we needed a house with an extra bedroom and a slightly bigger garden.

The printer

I'd just managed to finish typing some tv comedy sketches on to my word-processor to meet a deadline I'd agreed to. I gave a sigh of relief and pressed the print key. Nothing happened. My printer wasn't responding at all. If this happened today I wouldn't panic at all. I'd be using a computer – not a word-processor. So I could either send them directly by email or ask any one of a dozen friends if they'd be kind enough to print them off for me. No problem.

But I didn't have a computer at that time and had never even used the internet. And nor was I in a position to rush out and buy a new printer because I wasn't doing that well at the time. And as it was in the evening the shops were mostly closed anyway. I tried and tried to get the printer to work.

Then I sat down and said a prayer. It went something like this: 'Please God. It's me again – but I promise – no tricks this time. I really need a printer from somewhere and pretty dam.. er.. I mean.. quite soon.. if possible. Thank you. I'll just go for a walk now because I always seem to think better when I walk. But you know that already.. in your.. erm.. infinite wisdom.. And no God I wasn't trying to be sarcastic.. and you'll know where I am of course so.. right.. I'm going..'

And as I walked out of the driveway I saw a neighbour, someone I barely knew, on the other side of the road, walking down his driveway carrying what looked like a printer. I eagerly and rather cheekily asked the man what he was going to do with the printer. For some reason I just had a feeling it wasn't broken and he wasn't throwing it away.

It turned out he had just installed a newer and better printer on his word-processor and he was taking this printer to a friend who'd shown some interest in having it. I explained my predicament and the man had no hesitation in saying I could borrow the printer right there and then.

He even set it up for me and made sure it worked on my machine. He wouldn't accept any offer of payment and said he was glad to help. He then phoned his friend and told him what had happened. The friend said I could keep the printer as he'd just decided to get a new one himself.

Was it just a meaningless coincidence that I'd walked out of my door at that precise moment or what? And once again I concluded this might be a sign. In this case, a sign that I was on the right track in what I was trying to do as a writer. It didn't make a huge impact on my thinking because I already felt I *knew* what I was doing but it helped and this batch of sketches included a few I did manage to sell.

The phone call

This is one I've already described in my book, *Writing TV Scripts*, (Studymates 978-1-84285071-8) in a section where I was advising would-be scriptwriters that coincidences that happen in real life aren't always convincing as fiction. One of my brothers, who lives in Derby, went to visit one of our sisters who lives in Brighton.

Standing outside a shop there, he casually struck-up a conversation with a woman, from London, he'd never seen before, and they ended-up swapping telephone numbers. (Don't ask! It's just something that particularly brother seems to have a gift for.) Anyway – the number she gave him was for an agency hiring out office temps.

When my brother eventually called the agency from his house in Derby he was given another number to call. He didn't realise at the time that this number was for an office at the BBC Studios where the woman he'd met was currently being employed.

And, incredibly, she just *happened* to be working for the script editor who'd been assigned to work on my scripts for the series I told you about, *Growing Pains*. The office temp was busy when the phone rang so the script-editor herself took the call. As soon as my brother gave his name and mentioned that he was calling from Derby the script-editor assumed he wanted to speak to me.

But of course he didn't and couldn't quite believe that he'd dialled a London telephone number and been connected to an office where his own brother was currently working.

We all thought the coincidence was weird. If you'd just care to imagine how many people might have been shopping in Brighton on the day that my brother was there on a day trip and how many offices there must be in London – not to mention how many there are in the BBC Studio itself – you will realise what kind of odds we are talking about here.

How surprised would you be if you dialled a random number in the city of London and ended-up talking to a total stranger who actually knew who you were? Especially if that person was one out of the only three people in the whole city who'd ever heard of you? The odds must be phenomenal.

And I suppose the obvious 'meaning' behind that one would have been that the lady concerned was supposed to marry my brother and become part of the family. It never happened and I must confess that it never occurred to me at the time.

But who's to say that might not have been part of a Divine plan? A plan to provide me with somewhere cheaper to stay than a hotel whenever I was in London working on a commission? As they say, God moves in a mysterious way. (Don't worry I'm only joking – although you never know!)

The chance meeting

And here's another coincidence I described in that same book. I was on holiday in Florida and got talking to a very nice man from Slough. I had only ever really known one other person from Slough in my life – many years before when we were both doing National Service together in Singapore.

He was a man I'd liked very much at the time but as with most army friends, never thought of keeping in touch with. So in a rather weak attempt at a humorous introduction I said to the man in Florida, 'Ah. Slough. So you'd know Michael Binnington then?'

The man gave me a startled look and said, 'Yes I do. He's my best friend.' And I assumed he was joking but he wasn't. And he assumed that I was teasing him in some way but I wasn't. He thought that his wife must have mentioned Michael to me in an earlier conversation but we hadn't even said hello before that moment.

I found out later that Slough has a population of over 100,000 people. To the best of my knowledge I've only ever met four people from Slough. Two during my army service and the married couple I met in Florida – with a gap of almost thirty years between these occasions – and two of the people concerned just happened to be best friends.

I gave Michael a call and we've kept in touch ever since. Nothing startling came out of that coincidence but Michael is a nice man and I was glad to renew our friendship so maybe that was reason enough?

The reunion

This little sequence of events also involves Michael who I talked about in the example above and they happened at a time when I'd been thinking about Michael because I was planning the outline of this book. I've already reminded you about the sudden rush of coincidences that gave me the final push to get on with this book. This was part of that sequence.

I received a phone call from a man called Bob Collyer who, like Michael and myself, had also served as a soldier stationed in Singapore during the time of the Malayan Campaign in the late 1950's. I was pleased to hear from him, because he was another man I'd liked but it was forty-six years since that time so naturally I was surprised. It transpired that Bob, a Londoner by birth, was now living in Derby and had seen an article that I'd written in the local paper. That had prompted him to get in touch.

We got together to swap memories and I told him about a long-playing record by a singing group called *The Four Freshmen* that somebody in a nearby barrack room used to play, and how I'd never forgotten it. I said that if ever I heard one of the tracks playing on an old-fashioned radio show it took me straight back to those days in Singapore.

I said that when I'd completed my two years army service and come home I'd asked one of my sisters to buy this LP for me – for my twenty-first birthday but was told it had never been released in Britain. It seemed like a trivial thing to remember when there were so many more dramatic things happening at that time – like people being killed just a few miles away in the jungles of Malaya and us occasionally being sent out on exercises there.

And so I didn't think Bob would have a clue as to what I was talking about but not only did he remember the record – he still *had* it. Without me ever knowing, he was the person who used to play it. He was happy to give it to me and after forty-six years it still sounds as good as ever.

As a joke I took it to my sister's house and said, 'I'm sorry May, I couldn't wait any longer for you to get me that record, so I've had to get it myself.' I then added, 'You didn't try very hard. I got it from the very first person I asked.' And incidentally Bob and his wife turned out to be living in a house that my wife and I had looked at and considered buying just before they had bought it.

Then another coincidence connected to those days in the army quickly followed. When I told Bob how I'd accidentally made contact with Michael Binnington he said that he'd been thinking of trying to organise a reunion. Several of our unit had been Geordies so Bob sent an article and a photograph from those days to a Sunderland newspaper and included contact details.

A few days later I got a phone call from a man who had been one of my closest friends in Singapore. A man called Dave Hall. Dave told me how he'd seen the newspaper article in the Sunderland paper and got my telephone number from Bob. But with a hint of amazement in his voice he went on to tell me about the following happening:

The day before the article had appeared Dave had bumped into another Geordie he hadn't seen for over forty years. Perhaps surprisingly they'd recognised each other and talked about those long-ago days mentioning various other people, myself included, who they'd never forgotten. And then they'd gone their separate ways.

The very next day they'd each opened the paper to see their own photographs staring out at them, together with those of some of the other people they'd been discussing. And what kind of message can I get from that? Maybe nothing more than we should place more value on the friendships we have. Is that such a 'meaningless' thing? But these examples are all concerned with light-hearted and positive things. I've also had plenty that were the opposite.

The job interview

I've already told you how many different jobs I had as a young man and how I hated most of them. Well this coincidence occurred when I landed an interview for a job I actually *wanted*. It was to manage a small family business. The advertisement had said that no previous experience or formal qualifications were necessary and training would be given.

It said the company was looking for a young person with intelligence, initiative and energy. Someone who was honest and trustworthy. I thought I was just the man and wrote them a letter. I was delighted to get a reply inviting me to attend an interview.

And the interview seemed to be going very well for quite a while. I told the truth about all the jobs I'd tried and about my initial desire to be a professional footballer. I explained that after this ambition had failed I'd never had a job that I really enjoyed or that challenged me on an intellectual level. I said that *this* job might be exactly the kind of thing I'd been looking for.

The person conducting the interview seemed to warm towards me. And that was where my efforts started to go wrong. The trouble was I liked the man and wanted to impress him even more.

When he asked me about my education I could simply have told him the truth. That I'd failed my eleven plus exams (at that time the essential exams, taken at the age of 11 for a grammar school education) and been to an ordinary secondary modern school. But for some crazy reason I found myself naming a small and rather exclusive grammar school about ten miles away from where we were sitting and on the other side of town.

His attitude seemed to change straight away. I could see he didn't believe me and I couldn't understand it. The school wasn't *that* exclusive and in fact one of my own brothers had won a scholarship and been a pupil there.

The man asked one or two questions about my time at the school and I did my best to come-up with convincing replies. 'Were there any teachers there you particularly liked?' he asked. I thought rapidly and mentioned a couple of names I thought I'd heard my brother and his friends bandying about. Then the interview was over.

The next day I got a letter saying I'd done really well in the interview until I'd talked about my schooldays. It turned out that the nice man who'd interviewed me wasn't a full-time worker in the family business. He was simply a senior director who sometimes helped out with things like interviews. He did this because, as a full-time *schoolteacher*, he was used to dealing directly with people.

And where was he working as a full-time schoolteacher? Do I really have to tell you? And he'd been there for many years. Maybe it would have helped if I'd included *his* name in my fabricated list of teachers I liked – but I doubt it.

And how strange, that the very first time in my life that I'd ever told a lie about my schooling, I'd done it to a person who was working in that very same school? A school with maybe a dozen teachers at most, in a town of over 200,000 people. And he was looking for somebody who was totally honest!

So what was this coincidence telling me? You've got it. Not to tell lies. And please note: this was *before* I had that little misunderstanding with God over the cartoons.

But come to think of it – I probably wasn't supposed to get that job anyway because I *did* eventually get a job I really loved when I became a teacher (and a teacher was involved here) or am I just creating pictures from bathroom tiles again?

Playing around

This one would probably seem amusing if it was part of a 'Carry-On' film but it now fills me with regret. But it happened and I'm trying to be as honest as I can be without offending innocent people too much.

Imagine if you already had a steady girlfriend and were planning to cheat on her by going out on a date with someone else. Maybe you don't have to imagine it? But the point I want to make will still hold good.

Would you feel reasonably safe in meeting that other person in a quiet back- street pub on the other side of your own town or city – if it was on an evening in the middle of the week? Perhaps not – even in a big town it might still be a risk not worth taking. So suppose you decided to meet that person in a quiet back-street pub in another town – a much smaller place? A town say, over thirty miles away, and slightly off the beaten track? Wouldn't that seem much safer?

A married friend of mine had arranged a date for the two of us with two young women who were serving in the WRAF and stationed in Grantham. He'd met one of them at a dance-hall where he'd gone because he'd heard about the WRAF camp nearby. He'd specified that we'd all meet in a quiet pub in that area and they'd told him of one and given him directions. As he said you'd have to be paranoid to think anyone might recognise you in such an out of the way place, in the middle of the week, and so many miles from home.

As it turned out the pub was surprisingly busy. The bar was so crowded we couldn't even find seats so we walked straight through it into the almost empty snug. We stayed for a couple of hours before leaving to go somewhere else. Nothing remarkable happened and I didn't get on that well with either of the young women.

On top of which I'd spent most of the time feeling guilty and a bit worried because I thought a lot of my girlfriend and knew she was getting fed-up with my behaviour. I was relieved to find her unsuspicious the next time we met.

But a few days later, at the home of my girlfriend's parents I had a nasty shock when her father suddenly asked me, 'Have you ever been for a drink in Grantham, Steve?' I hesitated before giving an answer, wondering if he was just toying with me, before going in for the kill. But it didn't add-up because he wasn't that kind of man. He was straightforward and decent. The kind of man who spoke his mind clearly and honestly. Playing for time I lied and said, 'I don't think so. Why do you ask?'

His eyes lit up, 'Because I'd never been there either until the other night,' he said, 'I played there in a dart's tournament for my local.

The place was really packed and we had a great time. You could have been there. Pity I didn't think to ask.' Then he showed me a trophy he'd won, little realising I could have presented it to him myself if I'd stayed in the bar and not moved to the snug.

Not much doubt about what that coincidence was trying to tell me. I was just too stupid to listen.

The bad taste joke

The very first time I met my first wife's parents I was hoping to make a good impression. I knew they were solid working-class people who lived in a very pleasant area and I wondered if they'd think I was a bit beneath their daughter if they already knew how many jobs I'd had and the district I'd been born in. Not that I was ashamed of my birthplace in the West End of Derby. I had loved it there. But it did have a bit of a reputation amongst people who weren't Westenders. I suppose it was a sort of smaller version of the East End of London.

Anyway – when I actually met the family I felt even more unsure of myself. They all seemed so tall and fit and hard-working and despite my own confidence I couldn't help feeling a little out of place. I decided to play to my strengths and tell a joke. That usually got people to sit up and take notice. My wife-to-be, approved. 'Listen to Steve,' she said, 'He's brilliant at telling jokes.'

They all did as they'd been told and I gave a great performance that kept them gripped. I paused before delivering the punch-line which was something like: 'Well how was I supposed to know you had a glass eye?'

But instead of laughter there was a moment of complete silence before Maureen's older brother gave a little chuckle and said, 'Yes, that's funny.' He tried to encourage the others to laugh too. He was a very nice man and knew how terrible I was going to feel when it finally registered with me that one of *his* eyes was artificial.

Can you imagine how I felt for the rest of the evening as I tried to eat the food my future mother-in-law had lovingly prepared for us all? And no doubt about the message *that* coincidence was probably meant to convey either. I just wasn't the right person for Maureen at that time. I should have realised it and either changed myself to suit her or quietly got out of her way before it was too late.

So I've dealt with coincidences that seemed to be giving positive messages and ones that seemed to be more like warnings. Here's one that I enjoy recounting but which just seems peculiar.

The Cat

The pet we have at the moment is a rather skinny but healthy and attractive tabby cat. We didn't buy her or even choose her – she simply moved-in as a sort of foster-cat a few days after our own cat died. At first glance, this cat (who we called Tabitha, after the spin-off from tv's *Sabrina the teenage witch*) for reasons that should become obvious, is the spitting image of the cat we had before her – except that *he* was male. We called him Tom because that's the kind of cat he was. A no-nonsense, no airs and graces kind of cat.

Tabitha simply appeared in our garden a few days after Tom died. None of us had ever seen her before. We were all struck by her similarity in looks to Tom and then amused by the fact that she quickly started to behave like him.

She would, for example, climb on to the sloping lower roof of the house next door and peer into the slightly-opened bathroom window of our neighbour. To the best of our knowledge no other cat in the district had ever done this, except Tom, and now Tabitha. Our neighbour remarked on it because he wasn't much of a cat lover and had probably thought he'd be able to have a bath in peace once Tom had gone.

We had a very large garden at that time but the place where Tabitha chose to lie most of the time was on top of Tom's grave. It's true that the grave was marked with a tiny cross with the word Tom written on it but we'd seen no other evidence to suggest that Tabitha could read or that she'd known Tom anyway. And that was the *only* patch of bare soil that Tabitha ever rested on. Otherwise she preferred to lie on the grass under one tree or another.

Then after a couple of weeks some people passing by recognised Tabitha, lying on the garage roof this time, and politely asked if they could re-claim her. They seemed very nice people. They made a fuss of the cat and told us they'd been looking all over for her. They lived in the same district but quite a distance away. They came back with a carrying basket and took their pet away without a struggle.

But the next day Tabitha was back again and back to stay. The strange thing is we are not great animal lovers compared with many people and the cat's original owners would almost certainly have given her more attention than we've ever done but she's been with us for several years now and still seems happy.

I jokily said that she'd obviously seen the cosmic jigsaw-puzzle of life as it was 'supposed' to apply in our little area and she'd noticed there was a vacancy for a tabby cat in our family.

She'd decided to fill it. So was it just a meaningless coincidence that she'd turned-up out of the blue so soon after our own cat died and then started to behave like him? And what meaning, if any, was I supposed to get from that? I must confess I still can't work that one out. Except to suggest that any meaning in it wasn't aimed at me – but the cat! But if there was no meaning at all to these happenings there's still a strangeness to the sequence that doesn't seem entirely random.

And these are just a small selection of the coincidences that have happened to me, or involved me, over the years. But I'd now like to include a very powerful one that had nothing to do with me. This account was emailed to me by a nephew and arrived just as I thought I'd almost finished this chapter. Not that I'm claiming *that* as much of a coincidence. My nephew knew I was writing this book and that there'd be a section on coincidences (but even then there was still at least a one in twelve chance of it arriving when it did!) But anyway, here it is:

The reminder?

My nephew Louca, was recently visiting the City of Manchester for the very first time since he'd completed his University studies there around twenty years earlier. As it happened he knew that there was going to be a drama documentary, based on the infamous Moors' Murders that took place in the 1960's, shown on tv that evening and that came into his mind as he walked past the University.

In that same spot, many years before and on his way to be interviewed for a place as a student, he'd paused for a moment as the name 'Edward Evans' came into his thoughts. He'd been reading a book about this young man's death at the hands of Ian Brady and Myra Hindley.

In the book was a mention of Edward walking past the university himself. For some unknown reason Louca started saying a little silent prayer to Edward and saying that he hoped Edward was now at peace and being cared for in a better place. Then Louca went further and, to his own surprise, found himself asking Edward's spirit for help to stay calm and do well in the coming interview.

Louca also made a promise to Edward that if he was accepted by the university and moved to live there he would visit Edward's grave to say 'thank you.'

The interview did go well and Louca decided to open a bank account in the City for when he moved to live there. He made the arrangements by phone and a few days later received confirmation of these arrangements in the post. Obviously the envelope had been addressed correctly or it wouldn't have got to the house in Blackpool where Louca lived but the name typed above the address wasn't Louca Hepburn, it was Edward Evans.

Louca felt a chill at the sight of this and phoned the bank to see what had happened. They were as puzzled as he was. The letter inside the envelope referred to Louca by his proper name and the other details were all correct. They had no explanation at all as to how this could have happened.

Louca, only half-jokily, wonders if it had been a reminder, from Edward's spirit, to keep his promise. Meaningless coincidence or some kind of 'message' from another dimension? As I've said, more than once, isn't it a good idea to keep an open mind?

But can you really 'use' coincidences?

Which brings me right back to what I said in Chapter One about the series of coincidences that finally made me sit down and start writing this book. I said then I'd go into more detail so here we go:

I was doing my daily tai chi exercises in front of the television set and watching a programme called *One Hundred Greatest Musicals*. I was really enjoying it and disappointed that I would have to miss some of it because I had to go out. (I have trouble using my own video-machine. I'm the kind of person who needs written instructions to use a torch or flashlight)

Anyway I phoned my sister and asked her to record the remainder of the programme for me. She reminded me that she'd already recorded *Singing In The Rain* at my request so I'd need to bring two blank tapes as an exchange when I went to her house.

Later, when I looked for two blank tapes I realised I had a problem. I had over seventy tapes but all with stuff on them I wanted to keep. I realised I'd have to choose the two I wanted the least and thought this would take ages. I pulled out the first two tapes that came to hand.

Written on the sticky label of the first cassette was, *Singing In The Rain*. I was deeply puzzled. It wasn't my handwriting, nor my wife Pat's and I had no memory of ever asking anyone to record the film for me apart from my sister.

Singing In The Rain is my favourite film of all time and I'd first seen it over fifty years before. I could never understand why I hadn't bought the tape or recorded it long before this. It seemed inconceivable that I already had a copy without even realising it.

Anyway I put it to one side and pulled the second cassette from its case. I felt an icy chill on reading what was written on that sticky label: *One Hundred Greatest Musicals*. It was in the same handwriting as the other tape I'd chosen. I subsequently could find no other tape with that handwriting on it. And as far as I could remember I'd never even *heard* of this programme before.

If I'd *known* the tapes were there and pulled out both of them at random from a collection of over seventy that would have been coincidence enough but to pull out two tapes I didn't even know existed and at the exactly appropriate moment was remarkable. But that wasn't the end of it. When I told my sister what had happened she said, 'If you had no idea what was on those tapes and weren't keeping an eye on them, someone might well have taped over them. So take my tapes anyway.'

And when I checked my tapes later I found that although *Singing In The Rain* was complete and untouched, the other cassette *had* been taped over. Instead of the beginning of *One Hundred Greatest Musicals* I found myself watching an episode of the 1980's top tv comedy *Yes Minister*. At the end of that was a second episode of the same programme but as it ended Elvis Presley suddenly appeared on screen, singing *Jailhouse Rock* and we were on to *One Hundred Greatest Musicals* at the *exact* point where I'd phoned my sister to start recording it on *her* tape. It seemed uncanny.

A few days later I went to turn-on my computer but hit the wrong switch and turned-on the radio instead. It happened to be tuned to my local station BBC Radio Derby which isn't always the case as I more often listen to BBC Radio 4 in the daytime. The first words I heard from a presenter were something about 'life-coaching?' I then listened to an interview with a clairvoyant in which positive thinking was one of the topics being discussed.

What struck me about this was that I had been meditating and asking for guidance just a few moments before I'd accidentally turned-on the radio and one of the things I'd been thinking about was the writing of this book. Which, I hope you'll agree, is concerned with life-coaching and clairvoyance. Not only that but I'd been discussing these subjects with a friend who is himself a personal motivator and gives life-coaching sessions to business-people.

But I still hesitated and after listening to the radio interview, I decided to phone a writer friend and tell him about the coincidences I'd been having, and perhaps ask for his opinions on the matter. Why I thought of choosing this particular man at this particular time wasn't immediately clear. He's a very intelligent man with a great sense of humour so he always makes me laugh but I have several other friends like that and I hadn't spoken to *this* one for about a year. I made the call.

My friend's wife answered the phone. A lady I hadn't seen or spoken to for about four years and who I didn't know very well anyway.

When I told her my name and started to describe who I was she didn't let me finish, 'Steve,' she said, 'That's amazing.' Then I heard her call her husband to the phone. There was a kind of puzzled excitement in her voice. He explained that just a short while earlier he had said to his wife, 'I must give Steve Wetton a call. It's ages since we've had a chat.'

That finally did it for me. I just *had* to believe that all the coincidences I'd been experiencing must have some purpose for me. The one with the tapes seemed meaningless on its own and so did several others but taken as a whole it seemed as if someone or something was trying to get my attention and nudge me into taking some sort of action. I threw all caution to the wind and decided to trust my intuition.

I phoned the radio station and wangled myself an interview that would 'follow-on' from the one with the psychic by discussing the book I was planning to write. The producer talking to me about the interview said she thought that positive thinking might be too broad a subject to discuss in the time allotted and suggested I focus on just one aspect of it. Without any prompting from me she said: 'How about meaningful coincidence?'

And incidentally it hadn't even occurred to me that the producer might think my request to get some free publicity for a book I hadn't even started writing was a bit bizarre. I had somehow assumed they'd be willing to do it.

The interview went well and included a couple of enthusiastic and supportive phone-in callers. On my way home from the studio I called into a local scrap metal dealer's yard to ask about some items I wanted to get rid of. The owner's face lit up when he saw me. He already knew me as I was born in the area (and had once owned a scrap-metal lorry of my own – one of my many 'jobs')

'What a coincidence,' he said with a knowing smile, 'We've just been listening to you on the radio Steve.' Two tough-looking workers stopped throwing stuff into a skip to nod in agreement. Then all three men took a break whilst they told me about some of the weird coincidences they'd experienced.

I felt curiously cheered-up by this. That three down-to-earth, no nonsense working men could find what I'd said on meaningful coincidences stimulating rather than risible. And for days afterwards other people would stop me in the street to add their stories to the growing list. I'm sure I could fill a whole book with such accounts. But the important thing to me was that it was yet more confirmation that I was on the 'right' track.

A few days after this I was watching The *Wright Stuff* and you've already heard what that led me to. You may still not be convinced and that's fine. All I'm urging you to do is suspend your disbelief and give it a try. I don't think I've ever spoken to anyone about this phenomena of coincidences who didn't have examples of their own to talk about and that includes sceptics. Can you honestly say you've never had a few experiences yourself?

I think human-beings in general are actively *looking* for more meaning in their lives. How else can you explain that instant feeling of joy when you realise you've just recognised another coincidence? It's a very satisfying feeling. A throw-back to the feeling you had as a child when you really did believe in magic.

And that takes me right back to the sub-title of this book – the bit about letting some magic back into your life. I'm not talking about believing in Santa Claus or having fairies at the bottom of your garden (though I wouldn't *completely* rule out the fairies!) but simply in accepting that amazing things do sometimes happen – things we can't explain by logic.

Could a closer study of things like coincidences help your life to flow more smoothly? And if it could how do you set about it? I'm glad you asked me that. I *was* going to tell you anyway but it's nice to see you're paying attention. Here's a few suggestions.

- Write down some coincidences that have happened to you in the past (and email them to me if you like, at: steve.wetton@aber-publishing.co.uk, please include your name and contact details)
- With the benefit of hindsight can you see what messages, if any, they might have contained?
- Ask a few friends to tell you about *their* coincidences
- Can you read anything into those? (Without necessarily telling your friends!)
- Start to keep a written record of any new coincidences that happen to you for a short period (no need to get obsessive!)

- Can you see any patterns emerging or are they simply interesting but apparently 'meaningless'?
- See if you can predict a few future happenings from studying these coincidences – for yourself and others

What next?

Don't take any silly risks but consider making a few simple decisions to test out any 'signs' you think you might be getting. To see if a particular coincidence *might* be trying to tell you something. And, certainly for the first few times, only take decisions that aren't going to be *that* important whatever the outcome.

You will usually know when something feels 'right'. Just like I explained earlier, in the section on making decisions. If you sit quietly and think about it your subconscious mind will step-in and warn you what's *really* the right thing for you to do. If you then choose to override your inner *knowing* with your conscious 'ego' that will be your decision and you may regret making it.

Can you really imagine any so-called 'normal' person having a subconscious mind that tells them it's okay to get drunk and enjoy beating people up? And perhaps film themselves doing it on their mobile phone? Of course you can't. Yet some people do this sort of thing. They are not *all* suffering from some form of mental illness they can't control. The vast majority are simply being weak and letting their ego take over.

You'll know when your true subconscious mind is talking to you because it will only try to guide you in positive directions – in ways that don't harm yourself or others. Basically your mind is programmed to tune you *into* the world so that you'll grow and flourish. It makes no sense for it to be otherwise.

Maybe that's why few animal species kill their own kind, as humans are so prone to do. They haven't developed their egos to anything like the extent that we have. Unfortunately they haven't develop our variety of skills either. What a pity that we have the ability to use our greater skills to good effects and make our lives so much more comfortable but sometimes chose to do the opposite.

As I've said before there are no guarantees in life so maybe you'll get *no* positive results from this little exercise. In which case you can shrug your shoulders and forget about it. Hopefully you won't have lost anything by it and you'll have exercised your brain a little – including your creative powers.

On the other hand, if you *do* seem to be getting something from it then your confidence will grow and you should become more aware of things going-on around you – more able to fit the pieces together in a meaningful and positive way. And even if you only *think* you are seeing meaningful connections because you are making them up then what harm are you doing it if works for you in a positive way?

Remember what I said about creating pictures from random shapes? Sometimes the shapes aren't random at all – as with the 'magic eye' pictures and sometimes they are – as with the marbled patterns on my bathroom tiles. And it can be hard to tell the difference at first glance.

So maybe that's also true with more complex happenings. Maybe some coincidences are meaningful and some aren't but you'll never know which is which unless you pay closer attention and give things a try.

Using your coincidences, together with the other things I've talked about in this book should definitely improve the quality of your life. Can you seriously doubt it? At the very least you will become a more sensitive person who takes more notice of the things going on around you and surely that's not a bad thing?

So now I've told you why I wrote this book and how I finally felt almost 'forced' to do it. And I've given you ten important steps to consider if you want to improve the quality of your life. I'll repeat once again – you don't have to treat these steps as a complete programme for you to follow. It should work better for you if you're prepared to go that far but it isn't totally necessary. You can try any one of these steps in isolation or pick and mix as you see fit. Just as a reminder here are those steps again:

1. Change your attitude
2. Accept there *might* be a Higher Power
3. Set your goals
4. Prepare yourself for 'success'
5. Use daily affirmations
6. Try self-hypnosis

7. Make a fresh start
8. Learn to persist
9. Learn by experience
10. Make use of coincidence

As I've kept saying throughout the book. I've always taken a fairly laid-back approach to all this and I suggest you might do the same. This is a book about enjoying your life – not about 'winning' prizes whatever the cost. As a matter of fact I've always thought it's a bit unfair that people win prizes for being good at things. Isn't being good at something a prize in itself?

As a child at school I was always embarrassed to get a prize, just for doing something I was good at and enjoyed doing. I would have been happier to see the prizes go to the children who *weren't* very good at things and who had to do them whether they enjoyed doing them or not.

That would have seemed fairer to me. Later on, as a teacher, I always got slightly more pleasure from rewarding pupils for the efforts they made and for their positive attitude, than for displaying their natural superiority over others in certain areas of activity.

Yes I know that competition can be a good motivator and it can improve standards all around. And I wouldn't dream of trying to promote idleness. But we need to keep things in perspective and I think that few sights are sadder than a nice person whose vitality is being slowly crushed by constant 'failures'. I know it's an old cliché' but it really *should* be the 'taking part' that's more important than the winning. I truly believe the world would be a much nicer and happier place if we all tried to think a little more like that.

We can all be winners just by being alive and enjoying the experience – whatever happens. We don't need to have a league table to decide who enjoys seeing a sunset the most, or listening to a piece of music, or taking a walk on the park with someone they love. Of course we don't.

Competition isn't as 'real' as it seems to be. It really doesn't need to have quite such a dominant role to play in all our lives.

And when I planned the writing of this book I intended to more or less end it right there. But I've had so many strange experiences in my life; experiences that caused me to believe that there really is some 'magic' waiting to be let back into our minds, that I decided to include a few of them anyway. I thought it was a shame to leave them out just because they don't fit neatly into any of the techniques described in the ten-step process.

But as I'm not sure if they really belong in this book I'm calling this final chapter 'And Something Extra'. You may feel, as I do, that they tend to support the idea of there being a 'Universal Consciousness' or you may decide not to read them at all.

Good luck anyway. I truly hope this book will help you, as so many similar books have helped me. Just remember nobody can *force* you to be happy. It really is your choice. So why not choose happiness?

Points to Note

Step Ten

Making use of coincidence

❖ Carl Jung believed in meaningful coincidence – he called it synchronicity

❖ Jung also believed we are all connected by a 'Collective Unconscious'

❖ Are all happenings random or pieces of a cosmic jigsaw-puzzle?

❖ If something seems to work, makes you happy, and does no harm to others why stop doing it?

❖ See if you can make sense of any coincidences that happened to you in the past

❖ Try analysing coincidences told to you by friends (without offending them)

❖ Keep a diary of coincidences for a certain period

❖ Make a few predictions and see how accurate they turn out to be

❖ Try to act (with due caution) on any guidance you seem to be getting

❖ Make sure you are doing no harm to yourself or others

❖ Always try to act in the most positive way available

❖ Nobody can force you to be happy – it's your right to make that choice!

12

And Something Extra

YOU MAY REMEMBER THAT DURING MY brief phone-in chat to the tv talk-show *The Wright Stuff*, the host, Matthew Wright asked me if I was sceptical about psychics and I mentioned having a relative who's told me a few remarkable things. I was referring to my sister-in-law Kay.

I've no doubts that psychics can and do make mistakes (just like the rest of us) and some of them are so vague in their predictions that it can be no more than clever guesswork. But I've always been impressed by Kay, just as I was with Jayne Wallace who I mentioned talking to earlier, on *The Wright Stuff*. Sometimes psychics like these two can be surprisingly accurate in a precise and detailed way and this is what interests me. How do they *ever* get it spot-on? Could they really be able to tap-into that 'magic' I've been talking about? I'll just give a few examples to get you thinking.

My first trip to America

I'd always wanted to go to America but never been able to afford such a luxury. But training to be a teacher bought an organisation called Camp America to my attention. I applied to work in any one of the Summer Camps they run there. I was impatient to hear if my application had been accepted and called on my sister-in-law Kay to give me a psychic reading. She doesn't do it professionally – just for fun – but she's good.

Her usual method is to read tea-leaves at the bottom of your cup so if nothing else you get a nice cup of tea and a biscuit.

(And before you ask – the answer is No – you don't dunk the biscuit. She reads tea-leaves – not soggy pastry!) Though I'm pretty sure the tea-leaves just act as a point of focus – like the marbled tiles perhaps?

Anyway I told her I just wanted to know if I'd really be going to America that summer and what it would be like when I got there. She launched into it straight away and spoke without any hesitancy. It was almost as if she was reading from a book – rather than from the bottom of a tea-cup. 'Yes you will go,' she said, 'And you'll enjoy it very much – but it will be much harder than you expect. Long hours and not much free-time.'

Well – nothing remarkable there, I agree. Any intelligent person could have made guesses along those lines and got them right. But of course she went further – into territory that was far from generalised and much more risky.

She told me I would work, at first, for a man who I wouldn't get on with. He'd be younger than me but someone who acted older and took his duties very seriously. She described his height, his build, his colouring and his slightly unusual hair-style. She also said he would sometimes smoke a pipe.

Then she demonstrated how he would use the stem of his pipe to emphasise a point by waving it in the air like an academic might do. (And this was at least six months before I'd know if I'd even been accepted or not.)

Then she said, 'Oh dear I don't know whether to tell you this,' and paused until I insisted that she carry-on. 'You're going to be involved in a fight, and it will get quite nasty.'

I asked her if, by 'fight', she meant some kind of verbal argument but she raised her fists in a boxing pose and said, 'No, *you* know what fighting's all about.'

I reminded her that I was now training to be a teacher and that I'd learned to curb my temper. I was a calmer, nicer person and my fighting days were over. But she insisted she knew what she was talking about and said I probably wouldn't be able to avoid it. But then she added with a sigh of relief that I wouldn't get badly hurt.

And everything she said turned out to be accurate. I did go to the summer camp in America that year. I did have a wonderful time but the work was harder and the hours were longer than I'd expected. My boss was a young man with certain colouring, and a fairly unusual hair-style, who smoked a pipe; behaved in a slightly older manner than you'd expect; and sometimes used the stem of his pipe as a visual aid. (And how many young men have smoked pipes anyway in modern times?)

And although he was a perfectly nice and friendly man in many ways, he didn't seem to like me very much. I think I made him uncomfortable. Maybe it was just because I was a mature student and several years older than many of my co-workers and this made the man a bit wary.

Or maybe he could sense some of the more dangerous aspects of my personality. Things I thought were well-hidden in the past. I just don't know. All I know is that we didn't get on and since he was in a very responsible position where he needed to maintain his authority I don't blame him for finding me difficult.

But I consoled myself with the knowledge that Kay's warning had been a timely one. With her words ringing in my memory there was absolutely no way I would lose my temper and get involved in a nasty argument – much less a fist-fight.

It just wasn't the sort of thing a teacher did. And it wasn't the kind of thing I did anymore either. On top of which this man wasn't being *that* unreasonable anyway. So even when he made it clear he couldn't work with me anymore and was getting me transferred to another camp nearby, I stayed calm and polite.

I was, in truth, very disappointed – partly because it seemed as if my positive thinking attitude had stopped working and partly because I'd made friends with several of my colleagues and had an excellent relationship with the children in my charge. I really didn't want to be moved.

But still I accepted the transfer to the other camp and to another age-group of children, without an angry word. Happy in the knowledge that I'd at least managed to prevent part of Kay's prediction coming true – whatever else I hadn't allowed myself to get involved in a fight.

And that was a few days before I was attacked by the man I met in the canteen – the man with the likeable girlfriend and the flick-knife. And as you already know it *did* get nasty and I did manage to escape unscathed. If all that was random guesswork it was pretty impressive guessing.

And there's a nice little tag-line to this story. It has very little to do with the point I'm trying to make but it's flattering to me so I can't resist telling you about it anyway. One day the two camps got together for an evening's entertainment in a large amphitheatre and suddenly – just before the music was about to start there was a loud commotion in a section opposite to where I was sitting. Everyone turned to see what it was all about – including myself.

It was the group of youngsters I'd first been in charge of. They were waving happily and chanting my name. At first I was embarrassed because I thought it might have something to do with the fight but it quickly became obvious their attitude was relaxed and friendly – not in any way triumphal or aggressive. They were just pleased to see me and wanted me to know it

It gave me a feeling of great satisfaction to see the slightly puzzled looks on the faces of my co-workers and know that at least some of them would be thinking, 'Maybe this guy who punches people in car-parks and threatens to put them in hospital has a nicer side to him?' So as Kay had also predicted I really did enjoy that first visit to America. I've been back there several times. (And maybe my positive thinking *was* still working in my favour in the long run? So perhaps there was a point to it after all?)

The unexpected gift

One evening when Kay was giving me a reading at her house she started talking about something that was happening at that precise moment – rather than something that would happen in the future. She described how she could 'see' a man standing at my door, carrying a large, square box in his hands. It was some kind of a present for me.

I smiled at this because it wasn't my birthday and I wasn't expecting a delivery of any kind. Also I couldn't remember the last time anyone had simply turned-up unannounced with a present for me so I thought it most unlikely it could be happening now. But Kay was insistent. She said, 'When you get home just say to Pat, where's my present, and see the look on her face.'

I can't remember what else Kay told me on that occasion but the pattern was usually very similar. She would tell me perhaps ten or a dozen things – some very trivial and others more important – and almost always about half of what she said turned out to come true. I know what people will say. That anybody could achieve a fifty per cent success rate by pure guesswork.

And I agree if the details you are given are sketchy but as I've already demonstrated, Kay would often go into great detail. And those were the times she usually turned out to be dead right.

She told me the person delivering the present to my door was a man – not a stranger but also not a relative or close friend. She didn't know him herself but said it was someone I knew on a casual basis. She had no idea *why* the man was giving me a present and she didn't know what it was – only that it was in a square cardboard box and it was something I would like.

When I got home I asked Pat the question straight away without any preamble. 'Where's my present?' She looked slightly startled and said, 'Oh have you just bumped into him or something?' Then her look changed to one of slight disappointment, and she said, 'I wanted to surprise you.'

It turned out that a neighbour we barely knew, had been clearing out some unwanted stuff and found a large box, (a large square, cardboard, box!) filled with art materials, tubes of paint, paint brushes and so on. He knew I was a teacher working in a local junior school and wondered if I could make good use of these art materials. I certainly could. (And what he didn't know was that painting was also one of my hobbies.)

He'd brought these things to my house just as Kay had said and, as far as we could determine, at the same time that Kay had been 'seeing' it. He'd also made a second trip (unseen by Kay I admit) to bring several canvasses to complete the gift. And I was delighted – with both the gift and the way Kay's prediction had been proved correct.

The missing cheque

On another occasion Kay told me I would get involved in some trouble regarding a cheque and she named the exact amount that would be written on it. She told me not to worry because the incident would be sorted out without too much trouble. This happened a long time ago and I can't recall the exact figure Kay named but it was a very ordinary amount like £138.00 (Or £118.00).

And Kay didn't give an approximate figure. She didn't say, 'over a hundred pounds' or anything like that. She said the exact amount and asked me if it meant anything to me. Was it a regular payment or whatever? I said I didn't think so and promptly put it to the back of my mind.

A few days later a worried parent came into my class at school and told me she was having some problems with one of her children. The child seemed to be going through a bad time and was behaving out of character. (This turned out to be partly due to bullying from other pupils but that's another story and one with a happy ending.)

But anyway, the child had started to do annoying things to get more attention at home. And now seemed to be implicated in an incident regarding a cheque that had gone missing. I didn't ask the parent how much the cheque was made out for because I thought it best not to mention anything about tea-cup readings and predictions at this stage for obvious reasons.

The poor woman had enough to worry about without thinking her child's teacher might be going a bit batty! She thought I had a good relationship with her child and wondered if I could help without making too much fuss about it.

I decided not to question the child at that time but instead asked the worried parent to come back to my classroom in half an hour at which time I would be in the hall doing PE with the children. The parent could then search through her child's clothing and belongings undisturbed. I'm sure you can guess what's coming. The lady found the cheque just as I somehow knew she would and it *was* made out for the exact amount that Kay had predicted.

And when I was working on this part of the book I was told about another strange incident involving Kay. This came from my nephew Louca (the son of my sister Carol) the nephew I've already told you about in the anecdote about Edward Evans. (And also the one who features in the dedication at the front of the book.) This is what Louca told me on this occasion:

The sudden illness

Louca was just a little boy at the time of this strange happening and staying overnight with his grandmother (my mother) as his own parents were having a night out. At some point in the late evening when they were both in bed, grandma took very ill and was in great distress.

This was most unusual for her as, although she didn't enjoy the best of health, she was one of the bravest and most strong-willed people you could ever wish to meet. (Remember how I told you earlier a doctor had once given her a few weeks to live and she had beaten that deadline by twenty years? My brother Bill had said at that point, 'If somebody could bottle the kind of toughness our mother has they'd make a fortune.')

Anyway she was writhing in agony on her bed and told Louca (who'd been woken by her cries) to try and get help. He was distraught. There was no telephone in the house in those days and he wouldn't have known how to use it anyway. Also he wasn't sure how to get out of the house either with one door bolted and the other locked with a key. In a panic he started banging on the wall with a sturdy ornament, hoping to alert the neighbours.

This only went on for a very short time before Louca heard someone shouting from outside. But even then he was in a panic because he wasn't sure how to let them in. Luckily he didn't have to worry about it. The door was opened with a key from outside and Kay and her husband Bill (my eldest brother) rushed into the house.

They quickly sized-up the situation and used a nearby telephone kiosk to call for an ambulance. My mother was taken to hospital where it was explained she'd had a severe attack of peritonitis which could have been fatal had she been left untreated for much longer.

And why had Kay and Bill decided to pay an unexpected visit after bedtime? I'm sure you can guess, because Kay had experienced one of her premonitions. This had happened quite suddenly at her own house just a few miles away.

She hadn't been reading tea-cups or anything of the sort. She'd just been relaxing and doing nothing in particular. The feeling of danger she'd had was so strong that she'd insisted on getting her own two children out of bed and then into the car so that Bill could drive them all to my mother's house.

Kay couldn't drive and obviously didn't want to leave the children alone and Bill was looking a bit bemused so Kay wasn't sure he'd take it seriously enough – or know what to do once he got there. So she insisted on going with him. Years later I joked that our mother had been saved by the psychic cavalry.

And after writing about this particular incident I sent it by email to Kay and Bill who now live many miles away from me in Cornwall, just to check I'd got the details right. And that led to another strange coincidence. As they were both reading it on their computer screen they had a surprise visit from their daughter Stephanie. She was really excited about something and wanted to tell them about it straight away. This is the little story she launched into:

The lucky number

The previous evening Stephanie had been in a bingo hall and waiting nervously for one number to come-up. Suddenly all the lights in the bingo hall went off and the place was plunge into darkness. Stephanie said that she suddenly felt cold although the building had seemed, until that moment, to be slightly over-heated if anything. Then for some unaccountable reason she had instantly conjured up thoughts of her grandmother (my mother) and at about the same time she got a whiff of some old-fashioned perfume her grandmother used to wear.

The lights came back on very quickly and the bingo-caller apologised and said he didn't know what had happened. Stephanie started looking around her to see who might be wearing the perfume she hadn't noticed until a few moments earlier.

But before she could make any decision on that the next number was being shouted out. It was number eighteen and the one Stephanie needed to win a hundred pounds. Not only that but eighteen was the number of my mother's house – the one from which she'd been rescued by Stephanie's parents many years before (and of course Stephanie had been there too, in her pyjamas, on that occasion.)

Stephanie said with a laugh, 'I wonder if grandma had something to do with my win?' and that's when they showed her what they'd been reading on the computer screen.

And yes this could very easily be nothing more than an amusing coincidence. Stephanie does visit her parents quite regularly and no doubt she sometimes talks about her Grandmother but my mother has been dead for many years now.

And this wasn't ordinary reminiscing anyway – Stephanie had gone there specifically to talk about a strange incident involving her grandmother.

When Stephanie's brother John heard about this he reminded everyone that grandma had believed very firmly in an afterlife and also had the occasional psychic experience herself. This is the example he talked about:

Pictures in the fire

Grandmother had been convinced that her husband (my father – and John's grandfather) was about to die in hospital, despite the fact she'd been told he was doing well enough to come home the following day.

Apparently she was sitting at home in front of the coal-fire when her attention was drawn to what she later described as a coffin-shaped hole that had suddenly appeared in the black coal. This hole then filled with flames that flared-up, which made her think of the crematorium. This would have been significant to her since she was a Catholic who favoured burial and my father was a Protestant who'd made it clear that he would prefer cremation.

Anyway – after seeing this 'vision' my mother knew she wouldn't be able to sleep at all that night and just sat waiting for someone to bring her news of my father's death. When nothing happened for a long time she did go to bed. But her premonition proved to be correct.

The following morning, my father got out of bed, dressed himself and sat waiting for transport. But at some point, before the transport arrived, it appears he quietly succumbed to a heart-attack and died. And another strange thing was that, I had visited my father on the evening before my mother had her premonition and incredibly he'd made the same prediction to me about his own imminent death.

He had very calmly and clearly told me he would never be going home again. He was going to die in that hospital. Now this coincidence might all seem perfectly reasonable if he'd been in a terrible condition and obviously suffering and if my mother had visited him that night around that time and he'd told her what he told me. But in fact he looked pretty good and he hadn't said anything like that to her.

My mother wasn't able to visit every night anyway. (And had been told by someone at the hospital not to worry about it because her husband was doing well and would be coming home in a day or so.)

He'd never been bed-ridden during his brief stay in the hospital and could still walk around the ward quite nimbly and without the aid of a stick. He looked and moved like a man in good health. I wasn't even sure why he'd been taken to hospital in the first place.

But on the day of my final hospital visit, the last time I saw him alive, he quietly placed a scrap of paper in my hand and said, 'These are the hymns I'd like to be played at my funeral.' He wasn't lying in bed at the time he was walking around in pyjamas and a dressing-gown and planning to watch tv in the communal room at the end of the ward.

I had simply laughed and said, 'Okay – but why are you telling me now? You've still got years ahead of you.' And I wasn't joking. He looked fine. He'd been a good athlete in his prime and he'd always kept himself fit and active well into his sixties.

But he shook his head and said, 'No it's all over. I won't be coming out of this place alive.' When I got home and told Pat what he'd said she laughed and thought, as I did, he was just being a bit grumpy and awkward. And she reminded me that he'd always had a slightly droll sense of humour. I would never have told my mother about the incident and I didn't get much chance to tell anyone else.

I was given the news of my father's death two days later after being called away from my classroom by the headteacher. I was stunned and said, 'No there must be some mistake. I saw him last night and he was fine.' Looking back I suppose it would have made a good line in a sitcom if I'd then showed him that scrap of paper and said, 'See. His handwriting's not even shaky on this list of hymns he wants to be played at his funeral.'

But I never said that and I can't even remember what I actually did with the scrap of paper. At the time it was given to me it wasn't something I wanted to take seriously or keep safe so I probably threw it away without showing it to anybody else but my wife.

And if you think I'm being irreverent here, by making a joke about it, I assure you that neither of my parents would have been upset by that. They both had a sense of humour and they both preferred to see people enjoying themselves rather than being miserable. I'm sure they would have agreed with me when I urge you to choose happiness.

So with that in mind I'll finish the book with another amusing story but this time one that involves me directly and has nothing to do with premonitions. See if you think this might have a tiny touch of 'magic' to it or not.

Distant healing

For some years now, as I've mentioned earlier, I've practised a form of spiritual healing called Reiki. In common with Tai Chi it's all to do with tapping into some invisible energy force. I heartily recommend you to give either of these disciplines a try if you feel so inclined. They will almost certainly help to make you a healthier and happier person.

But back to my final little story – one day when I'd only been practising Reiki for a few months I was sitting in the canteen of Derby University when a fellow tutor started teasing me. She showed me her sprained ankle and said she'd been hobbling about in pain for several days. 'I want you to fix it,' she said. Then she added, 'Don't look so worried Steve. I know Reiki's a load of rubbish so there's no need to feel embarrassed when you can't do it.'

And of course everyone within earshot laughed because it was said in a light-hearted way and I wasn't at all offended. But I had a class to teach and explained I didn't have the time to do anything right there and then. That got another laugh because it sounded like a convenient excuse. Then I remembered something I'd been taught – that Reiki healing (which is usually a sort of laying-on of hands) can also work at a distance. It was an accepted part of the practice I hadn't tried.

'Tell you what,' I said, 'At half past three I'll be having a twenty minute break. I won't have time to go all the way over to your lecture-room, so I'll just sit down quietly for a few minutes and send you a distant healing.' And naturally that got another laugh – even though I was trying to be serious and really meant what I was saying.

At about six o'clock that afternoon I was walking across the car park when I heard someone shout my name. It was the lady with the sprained ankle and she was running after me and leaping about like a gazelle. She gave me a big hug and said. 'I still don't believe it but it worked. There's no pain at all. Thank you.'

I smiled and wagged a finger at her, 'Well you don't have to believe or disbelieve. Just keep an open mind. And that can be good enough.'

Which is, of course, something I've been saying to all of you throughout this book. I hope you'll remember it. And that wouldn't be such a bad note to end on.

Except that's not quite the end of the story. The thing is – I'd got so involved with my students that afternoon some of us had carried on working without having a break. And I'd forgotten all about my promise to send a distant healing.

So what had happened? Did my colleague just heal in the normal way? That seems a bit unlikely if she'd been in pain for several days without any improvement at all until that point. Was it what many people call the 'placebo effect'? Which means you've somehow cured yourself by believing you've been given a cure – whether you have or not. But isn't that in itself mysterious?

And doesn't it tend to support a what I've been saying about the mind being more powerful than we're sometimes prepared to admit? And you also have to consider the fact that, in this instance, the lady concerned *didn't* believe in me. So how would the placebo effect come into that?

When I asked a Reiki expert for his view he was amused. 'Who knows?' he said, 'It might have been either of those things you've just mentioned. But don't discount Reiki. You'd stated your clear intention to help her and maybe that was enough on this occasion?' Then he said, 'And I'll bet you anything it won't be the last time it happens.' He was right. Similar things have happened several times since then.

How do such things work? As I've said right near the beginning of this book. I simply don't know. I just know that they can and sometimes do. So I'm glad I decided to keep an open mind. I'm glad I decided to believe their *might* be a higher power and that we might all be psychic to some degree – and this might be a quality we can develop.

And most of all I'm glad I decided to choose happiness. I hope you'll decide to do the same.

Decision Making Chart

	Good at	Want to	Chances	Payment	Support	Total
Tv sitcom	6	9	4	10	7	36
Tv drama	6	7	4	9	7	34
Radio sitcom	9	8	8	4	8	37
Radio play	5	5	8	5	6	29
Stories	9	6	5	3	3	26
Stage play	9	5	4	3	3	24
Novel	6	3	4	3	3	19

Index

Liverpool
Community
College